Activities for including children with

Autistic spectrum difficulties

IDENTIFYING AND SUPPORTING NEEDS • ACTIVITIES COVERING EARLY LEARNING GOALS • WORKING WITH PARENTS

PLAY TIMETABLE

Choose

DR HANNAH MORTIMER, FIONA HOVER AND ANDY OGDEN

Authors
Dr Hannah Mortimer
Fiona Hover
Andy Ogden

Editor
Victoria Lee

Assistant Editor
Charlotte Ronalds

Series Designers
Sarah Rock/Anna Oliwa

Designer
Catherine Mason

Illustrations
Bethan Matthews

Cover artwork
Katherine Lucas

Acknowledgements

The publishers wish to thank Katherine Playford for the 'Tuneful traffic' and 'Dragon tales' activity ideas.

Every effort has been made to trace copyright holders and the publishers apologise for any inadvertent omissions.

Due to the nature of the web, the publisher cannot guarantee the content or links of any of the websites referred to. It is the responsibility of the reader to assess the suitability of websites.

Text © 2005, Dr Hannah Mortimer, Fiona Hover, Andy Ogden
© 2005, Scholastic Ltd

Published by Scholastic Ltd, Villiers House,
Clarendon Avenue, Leamington Spa, Warwickshire CV32 5PR

Visit our website at www.scholastic.co.uk

Printed by Bell & Bain Ltd, Glasgow

2 3 4 5 6 7 8 9 0   6 7 8 9 0 1 2 3 4

British Library Cataloguing-in-Publication Data A catalogue record for this book is available from the British Library.

ISBN 0-439-97188-8 ISBN 978-0439-97188-1

Activities for including children with Autistic Spectrum Difficulties

INTRODUCTION

Including children who have autistic spectrum difficulties can be both challenging and rewarding. This book helps you to put inclusion into practice so that all the children benefit.

Aims of the series

There is a revised *Code of Practice* in England for the identification and assessment of special educational needs (SEN) that has been published by the DfES, and this gives new guidance on including children who have disabilities. In addition, the National Numeracy and National Literacy Strategies emphasise the key role that teachers play in making sure that the curriculum is accessible to all pupils. The Government's strategy for SEN includes a whole framework of initiatives to remove barriers to pupils' achievement, and we are now beginning to see joined up policies that can make real differences to children. This series aims to provide suggestions to class teachers and others working in schools on how to meet and monitor special educational needs under the new guidelines. It will provide accessible information and advice for class teachers and subject teachers at Key Stage 1 and Key Stage 2. It will also provide practical examples of how they can use this information to plan inclusive teaching across the strands of the National Curriculum.

There is related legislation and guidance in Wales, Scotland and Northern Ireland, though the detail and terminology is rather different. For example, the 'Statement' of SEN in England and Wales is called a 'Record' in Scotland. Nevertheless, the general approaches and information covered in this book will be relevant throughout the UK.

Within this *Special Needs in the Primary Years* series, there are five books on helping children with most kinds of special need:
● *Special Needs Handbook*, which supplies general information for special educational needs coordinators (SENCOs) or class teachers to help meet all the special educational needs in the school or class
● *The Essential A–Z Guide to Special Needs*, which provides basic information for class teachers and support assistants
● *Activities for Including Children with Behavioural difficulties*
● *Activities for Including Children with Autistic Spectrum Difficulties*
● *Activities for Including Children with Dyslexia and Language Difficulties*
– these final three titles contain practical activities for including these children in the primary curriculum.

Including children with autistic spectrum difficulties

Most schools and classes will at some point include children who have autistic spectrum disorders (ASD) as more of these children are identified and assessed earlier. This book aims to provide a broad understanding of different areas of ASD and show how primary teachers can make individual education plans for these children. The

activity sections provide examples of practical activities that have an inclusive approach to meeting the needs across those areas of the National Curriculum most affected by any ASD.

Who this book is for

First and foremost, this book is for SENCOs, class teachers and support assistants who work on a daily basis with the children. The book will also be helpful for support professionals, headteachers and governors to use with the staff they work with. The SENCO's role is to support their colleagues in meeting SEN in their schools, though it is the responsibility of *each staff member* to support children who have SEN within their classes. This book will help SENCOs provide colleagues with general information about identifying, assessing, planning for and including children who have ASD. Finally, the book will also be a useful reference tool for parents, carers and trainees.

The children concerned

For some children, the whole process of enjoying company, coping with social situations, holding conversations and communicating effectively with others does not happen spontaneously. These children become more absorbed into their own worlds and agendas. They may use little eye contact, or even struggle to avoid it. They may join in an activity only if an adult insists and helps them. They tend not to play with other children, or may *want* to play but not know how to. They also have 'mono attention' or the ability to focus only on one thing at a time – often, if they are concentrating on their work, they might not respond to their names when called by a teacher. They may seem idiosyncratic, aloof and indifferent to other people, preferring certain favourite objects, toys or videos. If they need something, then they tend simply to go and fetch it rather than to make requests. Their conversations, if and when they develop, can be one-sided and the children find it hard to take on board the listener's point of view, talking about what is on their mind when the listener has no idea what it is. They also tend to use and understand language very literally, so that the use of metaphor, irony or figures of speech may be lost on them. They may carry out little routines and rituals of behaviours in order to 'keep the world the same', and they find changes to routines difficult to cope with. Their play tends to be repetitive and stereotyped, with little creativity or imagination. Sometimes children have both ASD and other learning difficulties, which means that they need highly differentiated and specialist teaching approaches. The activities later in this book have been selected for children whose primary difficulty is ASD and who are otherwise learning at the usual pace.

To draw this together, children with autistic spectrum difficulties have problems with social relationships, with communication, with developing imagination and play, and they are resistant to changes in routine. It is called a 'spectrum' because there are a wide range of difficulties that affect children in different ways. It can be a life-long

disability and about 80,000 people in Britain are described as being autistic. Early diagnosis and help is known to be essential in alleviating the symptoms of the condition. Children can demonstrate different forms and degrees of ASD and this book aims to cover the most common: children with autism, autistic features, Asperger's syndrome and semantic pragmatic difficulties.

How to use the book

In Chapter 1 you will be introduced to the concept of 'inclusion' as it relates to children with ASD. In particular, you will see what the implications of these difficulties are for the child and for the teacher at different ages and stages. You will also think about some of the issues and challenges that you face when working with these children. There are suggestions for assessing children with different kinds of social and communication difficulties in Chapter 2. Sometimes different types of difficulty might call for different types of assessment and you will be helped to select the most appropriate method for your situation. You will also find a description of the legal requirements on you to identify and support children who have SEN on account of their ASD. Chapter 3 helps you to plan interventions for these children, working with their strengths and weaknesses. You will meet a wide range of approaches that colleagues in other schools have found helpful and you will later be helped to match these approaches effectively to your teaching activities.

Six activity chapters follow and these cover the six strands of the National Curriculum which are perhaps affected most by this area of need. If a child has a significant difficulty in social interaction and communication, then most will experience learning difficulties in the areas of English 1: Speaking and listening, and English 3: Writing. Children with ASD who find it difficult to understand abstract concepts might find Maths 2: Number and algebra particularly challenging. Information and communication technology and Music can also be areas of particular strength and are therefore included because of the opportunities they present for the pupil who has ASD. Breaktimes can be particularly threatening and challenging for a child with ASD and Physical Education provides opportunities for teaching playground games and for developing social skills in less structured situations.

Throughout these activity chapters, you will find that words in italic

can be cross-referenced to Chapters 1 and 3, thereby serving as an effective 'shorthand' for explanations met earlier in the book. Though there may well be social and communication difficulties across each area of the curriculum, it is hoped that examples in these six strands will provide you with starting points and ideas necessary to help you deliver the entire curriculum in a supportive and inclusive way. There are two teaching activities for each age range of five to seven years, seven to nine years and nine to eleven years, each on a separate page. You will also find an introduction to each strand, covering how children with ASD are likely to be affected in that particular area of the curriculum and what interventions should help.

For each teaching activity, you will find a 'Learning Objective for all the children' and also an 'Individual learning target' for children with ASD. There are also suggestions for providing 'Special support' and for 'Extension' (what to try next for the children if the objective was met). The support suggestions link back to Chapter 3 where each approach is described to you in more detail. The activities have been selected to make a particular point for teaching children with ASD, reflecting the strengths, weaknesses, opportunities and challenges of those pupils. They should be adapted to suit the situation of each teacher and class and should act as a stimulus to trigger ideas and for the teacher to adapt.

Throughout the book there are photocopiable pages linked to assessment, monitoring and planning the activities and, at the end of the book, there is a list of helpful resources. You will find more detail about meeting SEN in the book *Special Needs Handbook* by Hannah Mortimer (Scholastic), also from this series.

Setting the scene

The activities described in this book encourage you to make use of a wide range of resources, materials and learning environments available in your school. Special use is made of circle-time approaches since these have been shown to be very effective in including children with ASD and in helping them to behave socially in a group. The approaches have also been selected to make children feel positive about their learning experiences and therefore grow in confidence.

In just the same way, as staff members, you need to be confident if you are to cope with the very individual approach that children with ASD sometimes need. The learning activities you plan should involve strategies for supporting these children that are workable and effective and should leave staff and children alike feeling positive. That is why this book has been written around a framework of inclusive classroom activities as well as a theoretical understanding of why we think children with ASD develop in the way that they do (covered in Chapter 1).

If you skim through the entire book first, focusing especially on the curriculum introductions and on the ideas for support, you will pick up ideas which you can transfer to different situations and different curriculum areas. After that, you may find it best to dip into the book as necessary, using it as flexibly as you need to.

Links with home

The revised SEN *Code of Practice* has strengthened the importance of 'parent partnership' and of good communication and joint planning between school and home. Usually a child's ASD is such that you need to plan SEN approaches for that child, setting and reviewing a regular individual education plan. In this case, you are obliged to involve parents and carers fully in the process. It is not always easy talking to parents and carers about their child's difficulties and you may find this easier if you can share some of the activities and approaches you are doing in class, discussing the ideas for target setting, support and extension which are exemplified in this book.

Overview grid for ages 5–7

ACTIVITY TITLE	SUBJECT	INDIVIDUAL TARGET	LEARNING OBJECTIVE	OUTCOME
TALKING HANDS	Speaking and listening	To listen and then carry out a simple action.	To use language and actions to explore and convey situations, characters and emotions.	A musical activity where different feelings are expressed through the beat of a drum.
OH NO, IT'S NOT!	Speaking and listening	To respond to a simple spoken instruction given to the group.	To take turns in speaking.	Children practise taking turns by repeating, agreeing or disagreeing with given statements.
RACETRACKS	Writing	To hold and use a writing implement with control.	To develop a fluent cursive movement for writing.	Children trace around a figure-of-eight 'racetrack' to extend their writing skills.
SENTENCE ENVELOPES	Writing	To write one sentence independently.	To write familiar words and attempt unfamiliar ones.	Individual sentences are placed in prepared envelopes for children to read and write.
I SPY	Number and algebra	To use their interest in numbers appropriately in a learning situation.	To understand a general statement and investigate whether particular cases match it.	A game where children must count the correct amount of an object and tap out the number on a drum.
CHUFFA CHUFFA	Number and algebra	To respond to 'add' and 'take away' using counting materials.	To begin to understand addition as combining two groups of objects and subtraction as 'taking away'.	Counting 'people' off and on a 'train' helps children understand subtraction and addition.
COLOUR IT HAPPY	ICT	To create a colourful design using the computer.	To try things out on the computer and explore what happens.	Children explore shapes and colour, using a computer graphics program.
MAKE A CARD	ICT	To use ICT to complete a simple set task.	To select from and add to information they have retrieved for particular purposes.	Children make their own greetings card on the computer.
PLAY THE TAMBOURINE	Music	To tolerate and begin to join in a large-group activity.	To play tuned and untuned instruments and rehearse and perform with others.	A simple activity where children sit together in a circle and learn to play the tambourine.
ECHOES	Music	To listen to sounds and make responses with a partner.	To create musical patterns.	Children listen to a percussion four-beat pattern and sound out a 'reply' with the same instrument.
CROSSING THE RIVER	PE	To join in a simple chase and 'tig' game.	To vary the way they perform skills by using simple tactics and movement phrases.	A game where 'wildebeest' try to cross a river full of hungry 'alligators'.
PASS THE BALL	PE	To join in a simplified football game with a small team of other children.	To remember and repeat simple skills with increasing control and coordination.	Two teams compete to dribble and pass footballs in this exciting activity.

SPECIAL NEEDS in the primary years: Autistic Spectrum Difficulties

Overview grid for ages 7–9

ACTIVITY TITLE	SUBJECT	INDIVIDUAL TARGET	LEARNING OBJECTIVE	OUTCOME
MAKING FACES	Speaking and listening	To indicate which of two puppets is happy, lonely, puzzled, and so on.	To combine understanding of emotional vocabulary with facial and body language.	Children learn how emotions are conveyed through facial and body language by watching a puppet show and then performing mimes.
QUESTION OR STATEMENT?	Speaking and listening	To join in a simple sentence-completion game.	To be able to form questions and statements.	Children practise asking questions and making suitable replies.
MIND THE MAP	Writing	To make a simple mind map and build prose from it.	To organise and develop different aspects of a character using a mind map.	Using computer software, children create a mind map of a chosen character.
GET A RESPONSE	Writing	To write a short letter.	To write an informal and formal letter with a purpose.	Each child writes a letter to a relative and then an embassy.
SHOPAHOLICS	Number and algebra	To turn a practical addition problem into a linear sum.	To learn how to do linear addition based upon a practical example.	Children role play choosing two items from a shop, calculating their total cost.
DRAMATIC MATHEMATICS	Number and algebra	To be able to match add/sum, subtract/take away, multiply/times, divide/share and work practical examples.	To learn how to recognise which of the four rules to use when faced with a written problem.	Mathematical problems are acted out to help the children find the correct solution.
INTERNET SURVIVOR	ICT	To navigate the web to find a simple piece of information.	To learn how to navigate to a particular website and to carry out a speaking and listening group survival exercise once there.	Children find out what survival equipment to take on a rainforest expedition using a particular website workshop.
EMAIL A LEG!	ICT	To communicate with one other pupil using email or e-discussion group.	To learn how to use attachments within emails to make up a 'Picasso'-style body shape.	Children practise emailing each other and create their own piece of artwork on the computer.
MUSICAL MULTIPLYING	Music	To chant a musical timestable.	To write lyrics to help learn the 3- and 4-times tables.	*One, Two Buckle My Shoe* forms the inspiration for children to write a timestable rhyme.
MUSICAL MOODS	Music	To use instruments to express anger, happiness and sorrow.	To be able to identify and express feelings within music.	Children listen to pieces of music and consider the emotions they evoke and then play mood music themselves.
BEAT THE PIT	PE	To throw a ball with approximate aim.	To throw a ball accurately underarm.	A ball is thrown into a hoop in an attempt to dislodge the five already there.
TRIATHLON	PE	To use a visual timetable to structure playtime.	To understand instructions and to talk about 'tactics' to use in small games.	There are three teams and three games. Each team learns one game to teach the other two groups.

Overview grid for ages 9–11

ACTIVITY TITLE	SUBJECT	INDIVIDUAL TARGET	LEARNING OBJECTIVE	OUTCOME
THINK BEFORE YOU SPEAK	Speaking and listening	To practise making a difficult request.	To realise what another person might be thinking or feeling.	Role play is used to explore what other people might be thinking in difficult situations.
BABBLE GABBLE	Speaking and listening	To choose an appropriate ending for a story.	To be able to retell a story in order and to choose an appropriate ending.	Children retell a story told to them and then invent a suitable ending.
POLICE REPORT	Writing	To record the key points of a lesson.	To develop the use of props to create interesting plot lines and help structure formal reports.	Children become detectives, investigate 'a crime scene' and write up a report.
IDIOTIC IDIOMS	Writing	To understand the double meanings in a series of jokes.	To understand what an idiom is and to know its real meaning.	Different idioms are explored and children create pictures to explain their literal and real meanings.
TRANSFORM-ING ROBOTS	Number and algebra	To calculate a simple algorithm, for example: 3 y = 9.	To understand how to use and interpret symbols in mathematical problems.	Simple algebra is taught by hiding the missing number behind a toy robot's back.
GRAB A GROBBLE	Number and algebra	To calculate in front of a large group.	To investigate prime numbers and factors.	A fun game where children record factors and prime numbers.
JIGSAW RESEARCH	ICT	To use ICT to contribute information towards a common goal.	To work within a speaking and listening group to conduct topic research on the internet.	Children use the internet to work in teams to research and write up a project.
THE WIND HISSED!	ICT	To produce a passage of creative writing using word-processing.	To use a mind map to assist in the drafting and ordering of a poem based around the use of personification.	Using mind mapping, the children create their own poem on the computer.
TUNEFUL TRAFFIC	Music	To compose a short passage of music.	To compose a tuned piece of music to known words.	Using notation sheets, children compose a short piece of music to go with the Green Cross Code.
DRAGON TALES	Music	To work as a full member of a team.	To compose music and perform a class assembly based around *The Snow Dragon*.	A children's book provides the focus for the children to work in teams to create a piece of original music.
LANDLUBBERS	PE	To listen to and share simple ideas within a small group.	To work as a team to overcome a variety of obstacles.	Teams have to cross shark-infested water, using only three 'stepping stones', and a piranha-infested river, using only a movable raft.
CANNON AND SYNCHRO-NISATION	PE	To take part in a PE partner game for at least five minutes.	To complete a gymnastic routine with other children a) one after the other b) at the same time.	Children create and perform a simple gymnastic routine in a team of four, practising cannon and synchronisation.

INCLUDING CHILDREN WITH AUTISTIC SPECTRUM DIFFICULTIES

Autism is a perplexing learning difficulty and several conditions fall within the 'autistic spectrum'. In this chapter you will learn how you can include and support the children affected.

Classic autism

Early descriptions of autism (by Leo Kanner in 1943) listed a number of features that the children displayed. It is worth looking at these briefly since, nowadays, those children who display them are often described as being 'classically autistic'. In practice, you may find yourself working with pupils who show some of these characteristics, though not all, and with varying severity:

- an inability to develop relationships
- delay in the acquisition of language
- even if language develops, it is not used communicatively
- delayed echolalia (echoing of other people's language)
- reversing pronouns (for example, using 'you' when the child means 'me')
- repetitive and stereotypical play
- behaving in order to maintain sameness
- a good rote memory (as if 'collecting' facts or labels)
- normal physical appearance.

The triad of impairments

Since this early description of autism, there have been many further attempts to clarify the particular patterns of behaviour and development shown by this cluster of children. It makes sense to do so, since it helps us be clear in our thinking about who these children are and what can be done to support them. It is now recognised that autism is a life-long 'difference' that cannot be 'cured' as such. However, an understanding of the children's needs can help us to include them fully in education and to help them function as best they possibly can in their social world.

Dr Lorna Wing and her colleagues at the Medical Research Council Social Psychiatry Unit carefully studied children affected by ASD and concluded that there was a 'triad of impairments' in the children's development. The three aspects appear to be as follows.

An impairment of social relationships

Children who are severely affected appear aloof and indifferent to others. Some may accept approaches by others passively but do not attempt to make social approaches themselves. Some may be willing to approach other people, but in a one-sided way, as if 'lecturing' at them rather than conversing with them.

Children who are only mildly affected may be happy to make social contact but lack understanding of the subtle rules of social behaviour, such as where to stand, how to show interest, and how to signal the end of a social exchange.

An impairment of social communication

Severely affected children may lack any desire whatsoever to communicate with others. They simply cannot see a point or a reason for it. With progress might come a willingness to communicate their needs, such as for a drink or a favourite video. Less affected children may communicate by making factual comments that might be irrelevant to the social exchange and therefore, again, rather 'one-sided'. Some children with ASD talk a great deal but pay no regard to their listener and find it hard to hold a reciprocal conversation.

An impairment of social imagination

For children with severe ASD, copying and pretend play are absent. They may learn to copy the actions of others (such as bathing a doll) but then play in a very repetitive and stereotyped way, failing to build on and extend the imaginative play. Children who are mildly affected may be well aware that other people have feelings and thoughts, but lack strategies for finding out what others might be thinking. People remain a mystery to them, as they cannot interpret the very subtle clues that most of us use in social situations.

What is the frequency of ASD?

We know that about 91 in 10,000 people of all ages in the UK are described as having ASD of some nature. The number of children being diagnosed with ASD is rising and there has been much debate about the reasons for this. Are we simply becoming better at assessing and diagnosing these children or are there other possible causes? Various suggestions have been made, such as environmental pollution, prenatal screening methods, viruses and immunisation. What we do know is that autism is not caused by poor parenting and that there does seem to be a genetic component. It might be that the disorder is inherited (ASD can sometimes appear within families), and it might be that the brains of people with ASD have developed slightly differently, perhaps as a result of environmental influences. It is most likely to be an interaction between many factors and much research is still being carried out. There are far more boys with ASD than girls: the ratio is about 4:1.

Diagnosis

Diagnosis of ASD is a medical matter since the categories of ASD are medically defined, based on nationally and internationally agreed criteria. Where there is good practice, diagnosis will be carried out in multidisciplinary teams and will only be made following a careful assessment of the child in many situations and over a period of time. Early diagnosis is important if children are to reach their potential, yet diagnosis of autism is rarely straightforward. More usually, you

will find that a child has been diagnosed with an 'autistic spectrum difficulty' or 'autistic features' rather than 'autism'. This is because there is a cluster of disorders most of which appear to overlap. In this book we have chosen to use the term 'autistic spectrum difficulties' or 'ASD' to cover the whole spectrum.

Diagnosis should always be followed by an assessment of the child's needs and strengths so that appropriate interventions can be taken. In practice, this usually overlaps with an assessment of the child's SEN and you, as primary school educators, will be part of that process. In Chapter 2, there is advice on how the SEN procedures should guide your assessment and monitoring.

There are different systems for assessing possible ASD and providing a diagnosis, depending on where the child lives. Sometimes this is done at a child development centre attached to the local hospital services. Sometimes there is a specialist autism team with multidisciplinary members. Sometimes it is specialists within the child and adolescent mental health service (CAMHS) who provide the assessment, diagnosis and advice. Since ASD can be such a difficult and traumatic diagnosis, there are also regional and specialist centres for diagnosis providing specialist and second opinions.

About ASD

This book contains the very basics of information about ASD. It is such a complex spectrum of difficulties that no one activity book can provide everything you need to know. You will find the recommended resources list at the end of the book useful for finding out more. The most insightful information comes through books written by adults who themselves have ASD and you will find these particularly enlightening.

People with ASD appear to see the world in a different way from others. Some researchers have suggested that these people are unable to draw together information so as to derive coherent and meaningful ideas. This is known as an impairment of 'social coherence'. It has also been said that children with ASD have a weak 'Theory of Mind' – that is the ability to understand that other people have thoughts and feelings and to understand what these might be. It is as if these children are predisposed against being able to make sense of the world or the people they share it with. As such, it is no surprise that the world can seem such a frightening and unpredictable place to them and that they display unusual behaviours. With this understanding, you will realise that many of the behaviours that single them out from their peers are related to stress reduction, frustration and a wish to keep the world the same predictable place. Many of the repetitive mannerisms displayed by children with ASD are deeply satisfying to them because of their predictability and the particular stimulation they produce. For

example, a particular child might feel a need to go round the classroom 'checking' each electric switch before sitting down. Children with ASD also tend to focus on the details and parts of information rather than to see and understand the 'whole'.

These are some of the most common difficulties that children with ASD share:

- Children with ASD find social relationships difficult. They might tend not to notice other people and so making friends is not a concept they can understand. Those with Asperger's syndrome may wish to make friends, but not know how to, and be wary of unfamiliar people whose reactions they cannot predict.
- They usually have problems with communicating or conversing using words and gestures.
- They find it hard to play and to learn in a flexible or imaginative way.
- They can also be very resistant to changes in routine.

Autistic spectrum difficulties are 'developmental disorders', which means that they can change over time and that they will both affect and be affected by other aspects of the child's development. In particular, if a child has learning difficulties over and above the ASD, you will see a very different pattern of development. Many pupils who have severe learning difficulties also have autism. Teachers and schools play an invaluable role in identifying whether a child with ASD also has general learning difficulties, as well as any islets of strength and particular interests. That is why full assessment of ASD should involve not only diagnosis but also assessment of strengths and needs. Only then can interventions be planned (see Chapter 3).

Asperger's syndrome

There are other children within the spectrum who may have developed language skills well but whose social understanding remains very poor and who show autistic behaviours. These children are sometimes diagnosed by a psychiatrist or psychologist as having 'Asperger's syndrome'. Rather than exhibiting stereotyped play, these children tend to develop intense interests and talk about these regardless of the context or the listener. They are usually keen to make friends but may lack the social skills to do so and these have to be directly taught. Even when they have learned social skills, they have a difficulty in generalising them to a new situation or a new friend or game. Their speech may be odd and pedantic, as if they

are older than their years, and the content may be centred around topics of intense interest to them. These children may have limited facial expressions and cannot use or understand non-verbal cues such as body posture or gestures. They may find change difficult to cope with and enjoy repetitive activities and routines. They may have excellent rote memory for topics of interest and they may be physically clumsy as well. Children with Asperger's syndrome continue to experience difficulties as they grow older, and

their conversation and communication tends to have an 'odd' feel to it and not to flow. Even as adults, they may have to work hard to remember social skills and to control their impulses to become tram-lined into certain routines.

Semantic pragmatic language difficulties

There are some children who have difficulties in understanding language and in using language in a sociable way or in understanding what is required of them in a social situation. These children are sometimes described as having a 'semantic pragmatic language disorder'. They may receive help through a speech and language therapist. The autistic-like behaviour tends to decrease as language and communication skills develop. Some children develop speech and language reasonably well, but have subtle difficulties in understanding the social nature of language and conversation.

Children with semantic and pragmatic language difficulties have difficulties both in the understanding of abstract language and in the social use of language. They may interpret language very literally and cannot cope with turns of phrase, metaphor or irony. They might stick to topics of intense interest, never wait for gaps in a conversation before cutting in, use poor eye contact, and become quickly distressed if they cannot handle social situations (like having to ask for the lavatory or asking for help from a supply teacher). They tend to take a long time to settle in a new-class setting until the adults and surroundings are very familiar. Usually, their understanding of abstract words is very poor (for example, 'quiet', 'kind', 'unusual'), though their understanding of concrete and literal words can be excellent.

There is still debate about whether semantic pragmatic difficulties form part of the autistic spectrum of difficulties or whether they are secondary to a language disorder. Regardless of this debate, your approaches will be similar and these children are therefore included in this book and the activities suggested for you to try. As with all learning difficulties, there are bound to be children whose behaviours and learning styles fall mildly into the category of 'autism', yet which have not been severe enough to receive help or diagnosis. You do not have to have a label in order to help, and this book should provide you with ideas to plan activities to help communication and social interaction for these children too.

Social difficulties

Sometimes it is helpful to see ASD as a difficulty in processing certain information. Children with ASD find it hard to process social and emotional information quickly and easily. They have to stop and work out what other people might be thinking or feeling. Simply slowing down and giving them longer to respond can be very helpful for them. They also find it hard to process social information while they are busy doing something else – they cannot 'change mental tramlines' flexibly. Some adults with autism report that it is impossible for them to cope with both the social demands of making eye contact and thinking clearly at the same time, and this

is why they do not look at others when they are speaking or listening. If rushed or 'overloaded', children with ASD may become so aroused that they can no longer think straight, and this is when you might see more challenging behaviour patterns. This is why some of the interventions in Chapter 3 are based around giving children with ASD a chance to reduce the loading on their arousal systems and calm down in a 'time out' area. It is also why new skills may need to be taught in a one-to-one situation with a familiar adult before the child is expected to perform them in a small group. Conversely, if you want them to perform well in front of others, they need to be doing something they are already very familiar with – coping with social demands and learning are two distinct tasks and children with ASD find it very hard to do both together.

Imagine it is your first day of work in a new country. You do not know the language and the customs. You cannot tell what others are thinking or saying about you. You are not even sure what your role is and how to follow it. There are people rushing everywhere, lights flashing, public announcements in words you cannot follow. You long to retreat to a quiet corner with someone who speaks your language and try to get to grips with where to go and what to do. If you can imagine all of this, you can imagine what it is like for a child with ASD arriving in your classroom for the first day. Depending on their temperament, they too may long to retreat to a quiet corner to reduce their feeling of overload. They might also want to forcefully scream and shout, or even to run! With this understanding, you can begin to see how the behaviour of children with ASD has roots both in their autistic difficulties and in their own individual differences. It also depends on whether they have general learning difficulties over and above their ASD and therefore lack the skills to compensate for their difficulties and learn new social behaviours.

The development of communication skills

If children with ASD are to learn how to communicate, they need to be helped to see a reason for communicating in the first place. Even if these children have developed spoken language, they may still have great difficulty in actually using this in order to communicate. Children, therefore, need to learn both language and communication if they are to overcome their difficulties as far as possible. In the early stages, children with ASD tend to use people rather as tools or pieces of furniture – climbing on them for enjoyment, leading them towards the desired drink, or hitting and running off when they want to play 'catch'. Sometimes, other children can be helped to include the child with ASD simply by seeing this behaviour as communication ('Look – Jamie doesn't mean to be unfriendly – he wants to play catch!'). Adults have to interpret this simple communication and turn it into a more appropriate language ('Oh – you want a drink! Here you are!'). In time, the child might be able to recognise certain objects as a cue to what might happen next (for example, a cushion on the mat to signal circle time). At this stage, 'objects of reference' like this can be used to signal what is happening next or to offer the child choices.

Photographs and symbols of activities and learning tasks can be used in a similar way, and the PECS system ('Picture Exchange Communication System') was developed for this purpose. Teachers have found visual timetables an excellent way of helping children with ASD to settle into a routine and feel safe in finishing one task and moving on to another. These kinds of visual approaches are used in the TEACCH programme (see below).

Different approaches

There are many approaches for supporting people with autism and

we shall look at a few most widely used in schools and in parent programmes. Given the wide range of needs within the spectrum, it is unlikely that one approach will be appropriate for all children. Some of the underlying principles have been adapted to form the educational interventions introduced in Chapter 3. Here are just a few of the approaches in use in the UK.

TEACCH

TEACCH stands for 'Treatment and Education of Autistic and Communication Handicapped Children'. This approach was developed in North Carolina, USA, and is often recommended by professionals for use in settings in the UK. It uses structured teaching, cuts down on the words used and makes the most of visually presented information. It can be used to help children with ASD make sense of their surroundings, predict what will happen next, understand how events are connected, become more independent and less frustrated. If you were following this approach, you would make clear visual boundaries for the child. The 'red table' might be where the child does writing and number and algebra, and it might be screened off from other learning activities, such as the computer table, so that the child has few distractions. Visual timetables would show the child the sequence of activities and events that session. The child might have a 'finish box' for placing completed pictures or work in, so that they know clearly when it is time to move on. Children are shown how to do everything rather than told. While you might not want all the children to be quite so structured and restricted in their learning, these methods have been shown to be helpful for children with ASD. The activities in this book will help you plan approaches using some of these ideas.

Intensive interaction

This is a way of learning about people and communication. It is based on how babies and carers learn naturally to respond to one another and takes the child back to this early stage of learning to communicate. It relies on mutual enjoyment of an activity, imitation, physical contact and a gentle running commentary. The adult uses bursts of activity followed by a pause to create an expectancy that

the child will respond. Rhyme, rhythm and timing are made use of, with the adult watching and waiting for a response. In this manner, a child can learn how to behave in a reciprocal way ('My turn, your turn'). Again, you will find that some of the activities in this book make use of these approaches. In particular, you will find that some use musical interaction as a first step towards social conversations and verbal communication.

Gentle teaching

Gentle teaching avoids using approaches which might feel punishing or aversive and uses rewards and ignoring instead. Because children with ASD are often highly anxious and easily stressed by other people or social contact, this approach has become popular in some special schools. The central strategy is to ignore or interrupt an inappropriate behaviour, then to redirect the child on to something more appropriate, then to reward that new behaviour.

Daily life therapy

In this therapy children with autism work intensively in groups. Dr Kiyo Kitahara believed that these children have weak emotions causing a disruption to their behaviour and learning. Children are taught to conform to 'normal' behaviour and development using highly predictable routines. Many of the activities in this book make use of routines and predictability to help children with ASD to join in and feel more secure.

The Lovaas approach

This approach, developed by Dr Ivar Lovaas, uses intensive behaviour modification techniques with children who have been diagnosed early on with autism. Most of the children follow intensive programmes at home during their pre-school years – perhaps 40 hours a week of one-to-one intervention for two to three years. The aims are to reduce inappropriate behaviour or any behaviours that interfere with learning, and to teach absent skills in a structured way in order to help the child develop and learn. 'Normal' behaviour is expected and any autistic behaviour tends to be ignored. In this way, it is argued, the child comes to learn through the systematic use of rewards and prompting how to behave like any other child.

Options approach

In the Options approach (or 'Son-Rise' program) constant individual attention is provided by parents and adult volunteers in order to help a young (usually pre-school) child establish relationships. It begins with a family-programme course to introduce the approaches to the parents and carers. It is suggested that, if adults accept and enthusiastically interact with young autistic children at their level,

the children will respond and become less isolated. Once these children come into school, their parents might ask that you follow a similar approach of setting high hopes, but not actually insisting on the required outcome.

EarlyBird

This is a parent training programme for those with young children whose ASD has just been diagnosed. It is gradually being taken up by LEAs across the UK to supplement what is already on offer and is usually available to pre-schoolers. Six parents are taken on each time to a 12-week training programme. Some of the visual approaches from TEACCH are used, and some approaches from the Hanen training for early communication (see resources, page 96). If you have families who have been through this training before joining your school, remember to tap into the training parents have already received so that you can build on it (or even learn from it yourselves).

What might you see in your class?

Each child with ASD is an individual, and the range of behaviours you might see varies widely. In general, children with ASD might demonstrate some of the following features.

- They often appear indifferent to other people and behave as if they are 'in a world of their own'.
- They might be desperate to make friends but lack the skills to do so.
- They may not play with other children and join in activities only if an adult insists and assists.
- They sometimes indicate their needs by taking an adult's hand and leading them to what they want.
- They may have very little language or have had delayed language when younger.
- They may not be able to follow non-verbal cues and gestures.
- They may find it difficult to understand the concept of feelings and may not be able to see another's point of view or appreciate that they have feelings.
- They may echo what is said to them or repeat a question rather than answer it.

- They may have a very literal interpretation of language.
- They may interrupt inappropriately since they are unaware of the subtleties of conversations and social turn taking.
- They may not be able to follow jokes, metaphor or irony.
- They may talk a lot about topics of great interest to them.
- They may become absorbed in arranging objects in a certain way, collecting certain objects, or spinning or turning toys repeatedly to watch them move.

- They may find it hard to 'change tracks' in their thinking.
- They may have poor eye contact or even avoid it altogether.
- They may be unable to play imaginatively unless it is in a very stereotyped way.
- They may show bizarre or very fearful behaviour, especially if familiar routines are disturbed or they cannot predict what will happen next.
- They may appear blunt to the point of rudeness, since they cannot understand discretion.
- They may echo your tone of voice and your words when telling others to behave – not in cheekiness but because that is what should be said.
- They may be extremely good at some things, such as doing puzzles, identifying numbers, technology, IT work, making music or drawing.

Welcome

We are looking forward to welcoming *Molly* into our class.
Thank you for telling me all about how he/she communicates.

What does *Molly* do when feeling happy?

What does *Molly* do when unhappy/bored/frustrated?

What does *Molly* tend to do when feeling anxious?

What usually helps?

How much help do we need to provide around:
going to the toilet?
dinner time?
playing outside at break time?
dressing and undressing for PE?
getting on with other children?
getting on with adults?
Are there any other situations where you feel we will need to offer particular support?

What are *Molly's* particular interests or favourite activities?

Thank you

Challenges and rewards

Working with children with ASD is one of the most challenging and rewarding jobs you can do in the field of SEN. Although this is a life-long condition, you can soon develop a knowledge and understanding of why pupils with ASD behave in the way they do and therefore plan interventions that will work for them. It is rather like learning a new language. Once you have learned enough about ASD to interpret the child, you have the opportunity to translate their behaviour for others and explain just what is being communicated. Never underestimate the intimate knowledge and understanding that parents and carers will have about their own child. Use your questioning to tap into their expertise so that you can 'learn the language' for a particular child as quickly as possible.

You might find it quite useful to write a letter of welcome (see the example left) in order to gather information.

ASSESSING AND MONITORING CHILDREN WITH ASD

Children who have ASD learn and behave differently to their peers, and each child is unique and individual. Here are ideas for assessing a child's particular learning needs.

Do all children with ASD have SEN?

Children with ASD may have considerable strengths and interests yet be learning and developing differently to most of the other children their age. Remind yourself of the legal definition of SEN, so that you can then apply this to your situation in order to help you decide whether or not the child with ASD should be included within your SEN approaches. Children have SEN if they have a learning difficulty which calls for approaches that are additional to or different from usual. If a child has already received a diagnosis of ASD, then there will have been significant concern over that child's development over a long period of time. Parents, carers and other professionals will have already concluded that additional and different approaches have to be used in order to match the child's very individual and different style of learning and behaving. These children are likely to need SEN approaches in school.

There may be other children in your class where there has been no diagnosis, but where you feel that there are social and communication difficulties providing barriers to their learning. If you are going to include these children in your SEN approaches, their difficulties have to be significantly greater than other children their age. In other words, you are expected to include a wide range of communication skills and social maturity within your class as part of your everyday differentiation – children's learning and behaviour always comes in many different forms and this does not mean that all these children have SEN. There might be one or two children in your class whose social and communication difficulties have persisted over time, and are extreme or unusual enough to demand individual approaches and plans. These are the children who have SEN on account of their social and communication difficulties and require monitoring under the SEN *Code of Practice* (DfES 2001). They may or may not have been diagnosed as having ASD, and this lack of diagnosis should never be a barrier to your planning approaches to support their needs. What matters for you as a teacher is how they learn, not whether they have yet been diagnosed and how they might be labelled.

What are the legal implications?

Your obligations under the SEN *Code of Practice* are described in the *Special Needs Handbook* by Hannah Mortimer (Scholastic). In practice, you are likely to be planning support through 'School

Action' if you are not working alongside outside professionals. When you plan interventions working with outside professionals, such as speech and language therapists, specialist teachers for autism or educational psychologists, this is known as taking School Action Plus.

For a few children who are severely affected by ASD, the support provided by School Action Plus may not be sufficient to ensure satisfactory progress in their learning. The provider, external professional and parents may then decide to ask the LEA to consider carrying out a statutory assessment of the child's SEN, perhaps leading to a statement of SEN for the child. Some children with ASD may arrive in school already with a statement of SEN because they have been statutorily assessed pre-school. Only children with severe and long-standing ASD or social and communication difficulties go on to receive a statement of SEN. A few children with very severe autism or with additional learning difficulties may be placed in a special school. Just because a child has a diagnosis does not mean that they should be statemented – it depends on the level of special educational need.

Target setting

One characteristic of School Action for a child with any kind of SEN is the writing of an 'individual education plan' (IEP). This is a plan which should lead to the child making progress. First, you should *formulate* a plan. You can then *implement* your plan over a period of time and *monitor* how effective it is in bringing about change. This evidence allows you to *evaluate* the effectiveness of your interventions. Your task is not to 'cure' the child's condition of ASD – it is to remove as many barriers to progress as you can.

An example of an IEP is shown left. This plan should be reviewed regularly with the parents or carers and seen as an integrated aspect of the curriculum planning for the whole class.

Individual education plan

Name: Carl   **Age:** 7   **School Action Plus**

Nature of difficulty: Carl has an autistic spectrum disorder. In his case, this means that he usually chooses to work and play on his own and becomes anxious if others approach him too quickly. He has a large vocabulary, but tends not to use this with people. He will often do excellent work (especially in mathematics), though it is usually when he feels ready for it rather than to request. He finds it hard to manage when there are large crowds.

Strengths: Carl has a detailed knowledge of road signs. He works well at the computer. He enjoys chase and catch games in the playground. He has an excellent musical rhythm. He can follow a visual timetable and also use this to indicate choices.

Professionals involved:
Specialist teacher for autism
Speech and language therapist
Consultant child psychiatrist

Targets for this term:
Communication: Carl will use a photo board to select a partner to work with.
Social inclusion: Carl will sit within one metre of the group at music time
Flexibility: Carl will wait behind a short queue at dinner time with adult support.

How these will be worked on:
Class teacher to organise photo board and music seating. Midday supervisory assistant to be trained to support Carl at dinner time.

Help from parents:
Carl's mother is going to help with the turn taking and waiting by using simple board games at home that we will lend out.

Review meeting with parents/carers:
Last Monday of term, 3.15pm.

Who else to invite:
The specialist teacher for autism.

Each IEP should contain three or four clear learning targets that the child with ASD should be expected to achieve with support. It should be reviewed regularly with parents and carers, and these reviews will usually be arranged and chaired by the SENCO. You can involve parents or carers more fully in the reviews by using the photocopiable form on page 31, or perhaps meeting with them to take them through it verbally.

Keeping children central

Children with SEN should become progressively more involved in setting and evaluating targets through their individual education plans, though this can be a real challenge when the child has communication difficulties. Just because a child has ASD, this does not mean that you are absolved from communicating with them about their education plans. Use your knowledge of the child and their ability to communicate to help them use their 'voice' in whatever way is available to you. Sometimes this will mean you, together with the parents and carers, describing and interpreting the child's behaviour in a way that makes it clear to everyone what the child likes, dislikes, is threatened by and is motivated by. Find out what the child likes doing best in school, what the child finds difficult, where more support would be welcomed and whether there are any worries. Sentence completion can be a helpful approach for some children to use (for example: 'I don't like it when…' or, 'I like it when…'). Other children will be able to select photographs to illustrate what they like doing best. Children with ASD will find it easier to give you concrete examples than to talk about their feelings. It always helps to keep children central to the discussion if there are examples of the child's work, photographs, observations and even video clips present for everyone to see and, hopefully, celebrate successes.

How can I get support?

Many LEAs are now employing autism specialists to help schools manage the complex and subtle approaches needed for supporting pupils with ASD. Contact your local LEA (ask for the SEN or Inclusion section) for information. These people often offer training and information and can also advise, either generally as part of School Action or arrange for specialist assessment as part of School Action Plus. The National Autistic Society (see page 96) also provides information, support and training for teachers, parents and people affected. Through the website, you can find out about various approaches for supporting children with ASD and this will be especially useful when you hear that a child joining your class has followed a particular method in the past.

Why assess?

For a pupil with ASD, there are two main reasons why staff might wish to assess:
● to gain information in order to plan teaching approaches or in order to plan a behavioural intervention – assessment must never be

done for its own sake and should always lead to an intervention that will help the child

● to evaluate different approaches and interventions in order to assess which are the most effective for the pupil concerned.

Within the field of ASD, there has been little agreement on a uniform and effective method of assessing children with ASD. The problem is that many of the tests that we might usually do are hardly likely to be effective measures for a child who finds any kind of social demand or imposed agenda difficult. If a child does not succeed in a test, how will you know whether this is because they lack the knowledge or ability or whether it is because you are presenting them with a strange and new situation that they cannot handle? For this reason, systematic observations and ongoing information gathering about the child in a range of situations is more likely to yield the most useful information. No one method of assessment or intervention is likely to suit all pupils with ASD, and each child with ASD is likely to need a combination of approaches.

What do I do first?

The first step with a social and communication difficulty such as ASD is to gather information through talking with the family, any other professional involved and through observing the child. When discussing this with parents and carers, you can usually find a positive way of embedding this information, for example: 'Kyle finds it very hard to play with other children and this is a shame because he is not enjoying school as much as he could. That is why we want to make a plan to teach him to…'

This is the kind of information you will need to gather:

● medical history, early development and background information from parents and carers, school records and colleagues

● general observation of the child including how they behave socially, how they move and how they behave individually

● a diary of particular problems and how you managed them

● an assessment of the child's attention, how well the child can focus attention and concentrate and when this works best for the child

● information about the child's hearing and vision, and of anything that the child is particularly sensitive to (such as loud noises or a preference for certain light patterns)

● an assessment of whether and when a child can use objects meaningfully and play imaginatively

● how well the child can grasp abstract concepts (such as weight and time) and understand spoken instructions

● how well the child can communicate their needs and the method used

● areas of strength that might indicate how intellectually able the child is in some learning situations

● whether the child can understand questions (such as, 'Where...?' and 'When...?')
● the child's level of spoken language (with examples)
● whether the child can follow non-verbal cues (such as a 'quiet' signal or your 'warning look' that you use for the whole group).

Sometimes a test of intellectual ability is carried out by a psychologist in order to assess whether there are other cognitive difficulties. Quite often a pupil with ASD will be able to demonstrate very strong skills in the area of non-verbal reasoning (for example, matching shapes and spaces), so long as they are interested in the test items. Verbal reasoning can be more limited with a definite gap in abstract understanding and the ability to think and reason flexibly and with imagination. However, this kind of assessment is fraught with difficulties in interpretation for the reasons we met earlier.

Using checklists

There are some checklists available to help with assessments of ASD, and several of these are available for teachers to use. If a checklist is standardised, it tells you what particular skills or behaviours are typical of a certain age or stage. Standardised behaviour checklists sometimes need a specialist to observe and analyse them, such as the ADOS checklist (Autism Diagnostic Observation Schedule) or the CARS checklist (Childhood Autism Rating Scale). You will find details of suppliers on page 96 and the catalogues themselves provide information about which checklists are available to which type of professional. There is a helpful observation schedule for children with Asperger's Syndrome in Cumine, Leach and Stevenson's book (see page 96). Sometimes you can use a questionnaire instead of an observation schedule, directed to colleagues or to parents or carers in order to gather information about a child's social behaviour and communication.

Sometimes rating scales are used to collect information about how a child with ASD is developing, performing or behaving. Training and practice in using these scales is important as so much depends on the interpretation of the observer. *The Preverbal Communication Schedule* (Kiernan and Reid) and the *Pragmatic Profile of Early Communication Skills* (Dewart and Summers) can both be obtained from nferNelson (see page 96). Though primarily for pre-school children, they can be used to assess early stages of communication difficulties for less able or more severely affected older pupils. *The Vineland Adaptive Behaviour Scales* are sometimes used to assess socialisation, daily-living skills, motor skills and communication, and are again available from nferNelson. There are details of an assessment and intervention schedule by Aarons and Gittens on page 96. This needs administration by an educational psychologist or speech and language therapist.

Designing your own observation schedule

Some schools have decided together which aspects of ASD they feel it is important to assess and have designed their own approaches. It is helpful if you again focus on the three areas of impairment.

Social communication
● Does the child respond when you say their name?
● Can the child take turns in a conversation?
● Can the child follow a simple verbal instruction?
● Can the child start up a conversation?
● Can the child change topics in a conversation?
● Can the child stick to an appropriate topic in a conversation?
● Is the child able to take on board the listener's needs and style?
● Can the child vary the pitch, tone and loudness of voice to suit the situation?
● Can the child respond to non-verbal cues, such as a smile or a frown?
● Can the child adopt the right physical distance from the listener to hold a conversation?
● Can the child tell an imaginative story?
● Can the child understand implied meanings?
● Can the child give a simple clear instruction to others?
● Do all of these vary according to whether the listener is a familiar person or stranger, or whether the child is in one-to-one situations, in a small group or in a large group?

Social interaction
● Can the child use gesture, body posture, facial expression and eye contact?
● Can the child play and learn in parallel to others?
● Can the child develop friendships?
● Can the child share an activity with a partner?
● Can the child seek or offer comfort when there is distress?
● Can the child imitate others?
● Does the child respond to social praise or criticism by altering their behaviour in any way?
● Again, does this vary for one-to-one situations, small or large groups?

Flexible thinking
● Does the child have a range of interests or one absorbing one?
● Can the child accept changes in routine or procedures?
● Can the child behave differently and appropriately in different situations?
● Can the child play imaginatively?
● Can the child accept another's point of view?
● Can the child generalise something learned from one situation to another?
● Can the child plan a learning activity ahead of time?
● Can the child suggest a possible explanation for an event?

Child's eye views
One of the most valuable assessments you can make is to use your knowledge and interpretation of the child with ASD and track them through 'a day in the life of...'. You can analyse a pupil's timetable to identify problem times and times when a pupil seems very

confident and engaged. It might be helpful to decide on a number of dimensions, such as how happy and confident the child appeared (with '10' meaning very happy and '1' very distressed or anxious), or how helpful the activity was for meeting the child's needs (again from '10' being very helpful to '1' not at all helpful). You will find a photocopiable version of this kind of observation on page 32. It then becomes possible to look back at your scores and decide on the

teaching activities that were the most effective and inclusive. Alternatively, if you have the luxury of an observing student or learning support assistant, a running commentary of a child's school day or session could be recorded as a way of getting across to others how you interpret the child's reactions to

their daily experiences. Children who are more verbal can contribute to their own child's eye views by making a dictaphone recording, taking photographs or writing about their school experiences.

Observation of behaviour

There are various ways in which you can observe and record children's social behaviour. When this is done prior to a behavioural intervention it is called collecting 'baseline' information. You will find more information about assessing behaviour in *Activities for Including Children with Behavioural difficulties* in this series. Here are just a few methods that are particularly suitable for assessing pupils with ASD.

ABC diary

Keep a diary of any 'unusual' incidents, recording what the child was actually doing, what seemed to lead up to it and what the consequences were. Write clearly and objectively, describing observable actions and using non-judgemental language. This is called an 'ABC diary' because it records:

A – the antecedent: what led up to the behaviour or what was happening just before it. (For example: 'Aled was experimenting with the measuring beakers in the sink. Tom approached him from behind.')

B – the behaviour itself: what actually occurred, recorded in clear unambiguous words. (For example: 'Aled scratched Tom's face.')

C – the consequences of the behaviour: what happened as a result, including what happened to the child. (For example: 'Tom ran off to tell me and Aled went on playing quietly.')

This allows you to gather information about the context of any unusual behaviour and, with the understanding you gleaned from

Chapter 1, interpret why the behaviour might be happening. For example: 'Aled finds it hard to cope with people invading his space. He cannot predict what they might do and this makes him frightened. His physical attack was his way of saying, "You took me by surprise – I was busy thinking, so leave me alone". I will explain this to Tom. I need to make sure I explain to Aled that two children can do this activity, and reassure him that this need not affect his experiment. We also need to do more work on being gentle.'

Behaviour charts

An ABC behaviour chart can help to identify any factors that may be affecting the child's behaviour. Like the ABC diary, it allows you to gather information about all kinds of behaviour and not to identify the problem behaviour in advance.

By recording the antecedent (what happened before the behaviour took place), the behaviour (exactly what the child did) and the consequences (what happened as a result of the behaviour), a clearer view of the context of the behaviour can be gained. For every entry of a difficult behaviour, record one occasion when things seemed to go better. This provides you with information about the situations which work well for the child as well as those which are not so successful. Both of these ABC approaches provide you with information about the context of the behaviour and any patterns in it. With your knowledge of ASD, you can then interpret the behaviour and plan the best intervention for it.

Fly-on-the-wall observation

Try to arrange cover or classroom assistance so that you can observe a child over a continuous period of time (for example, 30 minutes) and write down what the child is doing and how they are interacting in clear, unambiguous terms. Record the time in the left-hand

margin so that you will have an idea of how long the child was working in a certain area, with certain other children or demonstrating a certain behaviour. Later, you can look through the observation with colleagues and identify any patterns to the behaviour.

Assessing obsessional behaviour

It can sometimes be difficult to decide whether or not to intervene when a behaviour is carried out repeatedly by the pupil and clearly affords much pleasure and serves to reduce stress. You need to stand back and consider whether the behaviour is actually getting in the way of the child's learning opportunities or making that child stand out to the point where other children might tease or draw attention to it. Ask yourself who the

behaviour is a problem for and why. Consider whether the behaviour might become a problem later on as the child grows older and therefore needs working on now. Some children with ASD pass through phases of particular obsessions and, for others, there is one over-riding passion that absorbs their interest for years. Ask yourself what function the behaviour is serving the child. Perhaps it is

reducing anxiety when they are not sure what is happening next. This is fair enough and means that you need to work on giving them more strategies for understanding what is going to happen next for them. Perhaps it is allowing them to block out demands; this is creating a barrier to their learning and needs to be worked on.

It is possible for adults to use the particular interest or repetitive behaviour to good effect. A passion for dinosaurs can be woven into project work and even developed as a career. A passion for linear patterns can be included in mathematics and pattern work or in a star chart for good work.

Find out how long the obsession has been around and whether it also exists in other situations, such as home. What strategies are used at home? How do they work? When does the child engage in obsessive behaviour and – just as importantly – when does the child not engage in that behaviour? Armed with this kind of questioning and information, you can then go on to analyse the context of the behaviour and plan an individual intervention if you feel that it is necessary.

Choosing the best form of assessment

There is no hard-and-fast rule about how you should assess any social or communication difficulties in your class. Make a pragmatic decision based on your particular experience, resources and situation. The main aim is to gather information about where you started from, so that you can then gather evidence about the progress (or lack of it) being made and demonstrate that you are meeting the child's SEN. It is the assessment which informs your plan and this allows you to enter the formulate-implement-monitor-evaluate cycle you met on page 22. Without a clear starting point, you have no baseline against which to measure change.

The National Curriculum and Literacy Strategy

Teachers have been pleasantly surprised at the way children with ASD have adapted to the Literacy Hour. Children with ASD usually respond well to visually presented materials, a clear structure and to songs and rhymes. The small-group element allows the opportunity to work on the child's IEP and also provides the chance to practise

turn taking and partner games. Teaching styles within the Literacy Hour tend to use all forms of communication, with the non-verbal aspects of stories being highlighted as well as the words. There is also a clear focus on meaning, which is helpful for the child with ASD. Children with 'high functioning' ASD (who have no other learning or intellectual difficulties) can learn to read usually without difficulty, though it has been estimated that many are 'hyperlexic' – this means that they read at a higher level than they can comprehend. You will need to assess carefully these pupils' understanding of their reading as well as their reading accuracy. Sometimes these children find it very hard to predict or infer information from a story they have read and might miss the whole point of a written question or text because they have focused on the wrong element of it.

All children with ASD need approaches that are an integrated part of their curriculum and provide opportunities for:
- developing communication skills
- helping them understand social situations
- helping them be socially included
- encouraging them to be more flexible.

The Qualifications, Curriculum and Assessment Authority for Wales (also known as ACCAC) has produced a set of guidelines on the National Curriculum in relation to pupils with ASD (see resources, page 96), and you can expect more guidance from other education bodies in the future. There is also a range of support for teachers working with children with ASD on the TeacherNet website (www.teachernet.gov.uk).

In the activity sections of this book, you will find activities to serve as starting points in the strands of English 1: Speaking and listening, English 3: Writing, Maths 2: Number and algebra, ICT, Music and PE.

Parents'/carers contribution to review meeting

Name of your child:

At home

When does your child communicate best at home?

What does your child enjoy most at home?

What are the biggest problems with behaviour at home?

What seems to help?

About school

Is your child happy to come to school?

Are you worried about anything to do with school?

How do you feel about your child's progress at school?

Do you feel your child's needs are being met?

Health

How has your child's health been lately?

Is your child seeing any medical professionals?

Are you worried about your child's health or physical development?

The future

What would you like to see your child learning next?

Are you worried about anything in the future (for example, the next class or a school trip)?

What questions would you like to ask at the review?

What changes would you like to see following the review?

A day in the life of

name: _____

date: _____

Time of day	Activity	Usefulness	Well-being	Inclusion

key: rate each activity 1 to 10

Usefulness: 10 – contributes fully to the pupil's IEP
1 – not related to IEP

Well-being: 10 – pupil appears happy and confident
1 – pupil appears highly anxious or stressed

Inclusion: 10 – plenty of opportunity for interaction and inclusion
1 – situation led to isolation or avoidance

PLANNING INTERVENTIONS

In this chapter there are practical interventions that you can mix and match for pupils with ASD in order to build on their strengths and weaknesses and make the most of the opportunities and challenges that arise.

The purpose of this chapter is to provide you with practical approaches for a range of children with ASD. Remember that each child is an individual and that it is not possible to provide a 'recipe book approach'. Nevertheless, by becoming familiar with some possible interventions, you will be better able to plan individual approaches for the children with ASD with whom you work. Each approach is given a title that will then appear in the 'Special support' section of each activity page. In this way, you can cross-reference support models to actual approaches and have several ideas ready depending on the nature of the child's difficulty and your own context. No one intervention will suit all children with ASD and each child will need a range of interventions. For example, you will see immediately that some of the interventions are for developmentally younger children and others require normal levels of expressive language. Therefore, your *own* knowledge and understanding of the child's individual needs should inform and enlighten which intervention you select for which situation. The purpose of this chapter is to inspire your creative 'cookery', not to provide set recipes.

Working with strengths

Clear expectations

As with all children, those with ASD can behave totally differently in different classrooms because the expectations on them have altered. If you expect a child not to communicate, then that is what you are likely to experience. If you know that a child can communicate given time and opportunity, then use pauses and slow down the exchange so that an answer is clearly expected.

Encourage communication

At first, encourage and reinforce all attempts by the child with ASD to communicate, even if the timing and content are not entirely appropriate. For most children, communication opens the door to exciting social interchange – for the child with ASD, this is not necessarily so. You would not wish to put them off just at the point that they are trying it out. Give the child a stock phrase to use if they do not understand something (for example, 'Say it again please') – this can reduce everyone's frustration.

Familiar routine

Try to keep to a familiar and structured routine. Children with ASD find it hard to understand time sequences and they sometimes become anxious about what will happen next. For some children, this makes it hard for them to finish one activity, since they are not sure how to start the next. They might become 'locked' into very repetitive play in a bid to keep their world safe and predictable.

Giving feedback

Children with ASD need regular feedback on how they are behaving. Target your feedback directly to the child and make it specific by using names and clear, observable language, for example: 'Jonny is *helping* Mrs Ford. Thank you.'

Good role models

Once a child with ASD has learned to imitate, you can use this to your advantage when teaching social skills. However, imitating good role models will not be effective on its own unless the pupil with ASD is also talked through what is happening. For example: 'Look Amber, Laura is *asking* for the pencil and *smiling* when Rea gives it to her. You try – ask... now *smile...* well done, Amber!' Often this will mean putting children in different groups for different types of activity in order to get the best out of everyone.

Musical interactions

Many children with ASD love music and movement. You can use music time to encourage them to look, listen and join in. Some of the activities in this book use music in this way. You might also find a regular musical circle time helpful. Make sure that it follows a set format and familiar routine, allowing children with ASD to feel settled and relaxed in a large group.

Special responsibilities

Children with ASD tend to lack social awareness and it is very helpful to give them particular school or class responsibilities in order to develop this. These give the child with ASD very appropriate prestige in front of the other children, can assist inclusion if managed carefully, and allow you all to benefit from any exceptional skills and interests that the child with ASD might have.

Useful requests

In the early stages of communication development, in order to help children with ASD communicate with you, you need to encourage them to *show* you what they want. You should make it a little bit difficult for them simply to get hold of what they want independently in order to help them *communicate* what they need at whatever level they are capable of. If a child can simply get a drink by wandering off and helping themselves, what need has that child to communicate? But, if you anticipate what they want and offer a simple choice, then you are expecting them to point to, or reach for, their choice. This is a very early stage of communicating and can be

built on for children who have very little language. Later, you can expect an approximation of the word (for example, 'di' for the word 'drink'), perhaps accompanied by a simple sign. You can use this approach with younger children before rough and tumble play, too. Many young children with ASD love physical play and repetitive games. If you wait until you have the briefest of eye contact before repeating an enjoyable action (such as a game of 'tig'), you have again taught them to begin to communicate what they want.

Use ICT
Computers are an effective means of learning and recording for children with ASD, since they are visual, predictable, make no social demands and are intrinsically rewarding. Sharing computers can provide an opportunity for introducing a social element, as can the introduction of emailing and discussion groups. Some children with ASD have been able to contribute very effectively to class topic work through searching the web.

Visual timetables
You can help by showing the child pictures or symbols about what is happening next. Make a series of cards with Velcro backs which can be arranged in line on a felt board, or use a whiteboard to talk about and draw the session's timetable at its beginning. You can also help by providing the words for what the child is doing. Do this by giving a simple commentary about what is happening in the pictures, for example: 'Joseph is writing' or, 'Zoe is putting away'.

Widening their interests
Sometimes children with ASD have intense interests in certain items or topics. For example, they might be fascinated by trains and tracks; they might be intensely interested in switches and all things electrical; they might cling on to two oblong bricks and stare at these intently as they arrange them meticulously in line; they might insist on carrying a certain blue toy everywhere. Try to be interested in their interests but introduce new things, too. Provide a special place to put the toy when the child is using hands for something else. Introduce cars to the train mat. Help the child extend their fascination in bricks to building and simple construction play. Try to support their activities, but also help them develop more flexible interests. Distract them if they become too absorbed or obsessed with their interests when this gets in the way of their learning.

Working with weaknesses
Avoid ambiguity
Children with ASD find it hard to understand double meaning, sarcasm or irony, and may interpret it too literally and become confused. Avoid requests such as, 'Would you like to do your writing now?' (The honest answer might be 'No' and, for a child with ASD, this would not be cheekiness!) Replace this with, for example: '*Rowan – please*

do your *writing* now.' If children with ASD begin to echo what you have said or resort to repetitive behaviour, this could be a sign that they have not understood you and are beginning to feel stressed. Make sure that your instructions are concrete, direct and explicit, and support these with picture prompts if you need to.

Being patient

You may need to wait longer than usual before a child responds to what you have asked for. Give a child with ASD time to respond or to imitate before you come in with a repetition or the answer. Sometimes these children need longer than usual to process what you have just said or shown them before they can then put together their response. Sometimes simple signing is used in order to make instructions and requests clearer.

Careful questioning

Questions often confuse children with ASD. They may not understand the question word itself (what, why, where, when) and they find it hard to handle open-ended questions. Where possible, turn questions into statements with a pause at the appropriate moment, for example: 'The colour of the leaves is…' rather than, 'What colour are the leaves?' You might also find the child echoing a question such as: 'Do you want the scissors?' when they really mean, 'I want the scissors.' You need to recognise the intent in the words and be ready to oblige with your own re-statement: 'Oh – you want the scissors. Here you are.'

Communication book

Provide plenty of encouragement whenever the child communicates with you, whether they have done so with their voice or their actions. The child might use unusual signals and behaviours to indicate a need, so you should put together a communication book to help other adults in your school understand, too. By now, because you have worked alongside and observed the child, you will be familiar with their patterns of behaviour and communication. You might start with:
This is how Adam shows us he is relaxed…
This is how Ashish shows us he is anxious…
This is how Freya shows us she is bored…
This is how Grant shows us he needs time in the quiet corner…

Developing scripts

Children with ASD are often at a loss as to what to say in certain social situations and may end up disrupting them instead. Use your observations to identify these situations and help the child rehearse what to say (for example, how to ask another child to lend something, how to ask someone to play with them, what to say at the staff-room door). In a similar way, you can make up stories to illustrate a social point and use them to demonstrate to the child with ASD how to behave in that situation. Remember that the child might not be able to generalise and apply what has been learned in

the story to a real-life situation unless you help them and remind them. Scripts and social stories can also be used with the other children in order to explain a particularly alarming episode of behaviour on the part of the child with ASD. For example, 'There was a young tiger who did not understand how to tell his friends when he was upset. So when… he would… and, in time, his friends understood that…' and so on.

Distraction

When it comes to obsessive behaviour, you will already know when the child with ASD is most likely to need the security of their repetitive behaviour. Plan ahead for difficult times by distracting the child on to something different and making it clear to the child what is going to happen next. Distracting the child on to a preferred and more appropriate activity also allows you to direct your attention to the other children's learning. Do not be afraid to sandwich structured teaching for the children with ASD with periods when they are engaged with a free activity, in order to share your own time better with the other children.

Engaging attention

Children with autistic difficulties are sometimes felt to be deaf because they pay little attention to spoken instructions. Use their names clearly, get down to their level, try to encourage eye contact albeit briefly (to signal your intent to communicate) and then speak. Encourage but do not actually teach eye contact (since for some children it makes them too aroused and prevents them from thinking clearly). When you are issuing instructions to the whole class, address the child with ASD by name first to engage attention. Give very clear and simple messages, showing the child what to do as well as telling them.

Finish box

Make sure that the child with ASD knows clearly what the learning tasks are. Break them down into discrete steps if you have to, and encourage the child to work from left to right with a 'finish box' to the right-hand side. Some children with ASD tend to perseverate in their behaviour, so as not to finish a task because uncertainty about what will happen next is so stressful for them.

Keep it concrete

Children with autistic difficulties often have problems in understanding personal pronouns such as 'me' and 'you'. It is often helpful to use real names such as, 'Give it to Molly' rather than, 'Give it to me'. They also find it hard to understand question words such as, 'What?' and, 'Why?' This is why you sometimes hear them provide rather unusual and irrelevant answers. The speech and language therapist will usually help the child step by step towards understanding more abstract words, and you could follow these ideas, too. In the meantime, you may have to keep your communications more concrete, showing as well as telling.

Motivators

One of the challenges in teaching young children with ASD is that they may not be motivated by social rewards alone. Praise might be meaningless, your gaze might be unsettling to them and the chance to play with other children might be something definitely to be avoided. Therefore, it is sometimes appropriate to use more concrete motivators for children with ASD, such as a favourite item to collect or a 'well done!' picture card. Always pair these with social praise so that, in time, the child comes to see the praise as rewarding as well. You can also make sure the work itself is intrinsically motivating for a child with ASD by appealing to any appropriate areas of interests (for example, dinosaurs or sport) when selecting topics, themes and tasks. Usually, these children need individually set tasks at first in order to work with their areas of interest and 'get them going'. You can add extra motivators that can be used as tokens for good behaviour – stickers, a favourite activity or time with a favourite toy.

Picture exchange

Sometimes children are taught to exchange pictures or symbols in order to make their needs known more clearly. This approach has been used in many schools working with children who have ASD. A contact address for PECS (Picture Exchange Communication System) is given on page 96. In this system, children learn to present picture or symbol cards to an adult in order to say what they would like next – perhaps a 'drink' or to work at the 'computer'. In time, these cards can be used to give the child a range of choices. You can adapt this approach using photographs.

Self-monitoring

Children with ASD are slow to develop social skills and might behave in a socially inappropriate way until someone from outside steps in to stop them. Focus their attentions on to what it is they should be doing that is more appropriate. You can then help a child monitor their own behaviour, meeting regularly with the child to evaluate progress. You will find a photocopiable monitoring sheet on page 44. This sheet can be used either for self-monitoring (where the child issues points to themselves, sharing the points with you and telling you how they felt they did) or for teacher feedback (where the teacher gives the points and explains them to the child).

Social mentoring

Pair a member of staff with a child who has ASD and arrange for them to meet together, so that the adult can help the child monitor their own social behaviour and progress, sharing helpful advice along the way. Some schools pair many of the children up with learning mentors who are recruited from outside helpers who have been specially selected and vetted.

Social skills training

Children with ASD may need to be taught social skills directly because they cannot pick up incidentally all the subtle clues needed

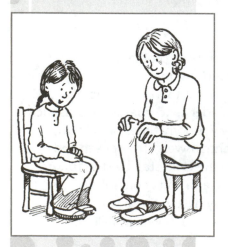

to manage a social exchange. The focus of your approach should be on telling the child what to do, rather than what not to do.

Take two

This allows you to give the child with ASD a second chance to practise an appropriate behaviour. If a situation has gone badly wrong because of a child's inappropriate social behaviour, try making your own clapperboard for 'take two', give clear directions and rerun the scene again. Because children with ASD are so visual, video clips can work well as a means of teaching appropriate social behaviour.

Taped texts

Some children with ASD find it hard to extract meaning when they are reading. Record the text on to tape and allow the child to play it back repeatedly until the sense becomes clearer. In the best of all possible worlds, a workstation at the side of the room with a soundproofed booth makes this a very workable approach. In the case of children with ASD who find it easiest to read and think out loud, it also allows the other children to work without this distraction. Taped texts can also be used to talk children through a set procedure or a new activity, and can be replayed until a child with ASD has grasped what is to be done.

Teaching communication skills

Any speech and language therapist involved might be able to advise you on the best ways of doing this for the child. The majority of therapists will argue that the best therapy is delivered through the adults most involved with the child, since communication has to be generalised to the actual social situations that the child lives and works in. Individual therapy might work beautifully in a one-to-one situation, but there is no guarantee for children with ASD that the new skills will be transferred. You can actually practise where to stand when holding a conversation, and what tone and volume of voice to use for different situations.

You may find it helpful to try the following game during *circle time* to help children control the volumes and tones of their voices. The teacher asks the questions and the children reply in different tones of voice. The style of voice can then be referred to later in the school day in order to help the child with ASD develop different 'voices'.

Have you got your quiet voices?
Yes we have, we really have!

Have you got your loud voices?
YES WE HAVE, WE REALLY HAVE!

Have you got your cross voices?
Yes we have, we really have!

Have you got your happy voices?
Yes we have, we really have!

Teach turn taking

It is worth spending some time teaching turn taking in small groups or with partners in the early days of the school year. Even if a child with ASD mastered this before, the skill can change as soon as there is a new situation or new people involved. Board games are an excellent way of doing this, since they usually involve logical and predictable steps. Give the other children clear instructions on what to do if the child with ASD becomes stressed. For example: 'If Leo turns the board over, give him a moment to feel calm again and then try just one more time.'

Traffic lights

This can be a helpful visual approach for children with ASD. Have a set of traffic lights (invent you own system) and flash up amber as a warning to quieten down and red as a sign to stop. When everyone has quietened down, redirect them again. Another use of this approach is when older children are given amber or red cards to display if they are feeling overloaded and need to take some time out to calm down.

Transfer objects

Children with ASD sometimes have a genuine difficulty in moving from one area to another – for example, coming from home into school or entering the large assembly hall. By giving them a transfer object (such as something to give to a teacher or a cushion to sit on in assembly), you can calm these moments down for them. Giving children a definite job to do in a new situation helps in a similar way (such as fetching a chair for the teacher).

Using a key worker

Start by helping the child feel settled by learning one to one with a familiar and supportive adult or 'key worker'. This is one adult who will be responsible for supporting the child through their school day and, in practice, is often a learning support assistant allocated to the child with ASD. Children with ASD tend to find adults more predictable and therefore more secure than other children at first.

For younger children, that worker can begin by simply working or playing in parallel to the child, observing how they are behaving, placing objects of interest near to them, and gently leading the child when new instructions are needed (such as for outdoor playtime). As the adult becomes familiar with the child's routines and behaviours, it will become possible for that person to predict what the child will do next and to begin to 'see the world through the child's eyes'. Gradually one or more other children can be involved in the work or play, with the key worker staying close to support and assist. The adult, having gained a feel for what the child will do, can interpret the child's play to other children and thus include them in the play. The key worker is acting as a 'bridge' for the child and helping them become more sociable, rather than acting as a 'shadow' (which can isolate a child still further).

Working with opportunities

Buddy systems

Pair children who are good role models with younger children for breaktimes and certain activities, especially where the younger children lack social skills and may be frightened by any lack of structure. Giving the partners a definite game to play or job to do can add structure to the situation, as can playground games with clear rules (such as 'tig'). In the activity section on PE, you will find some ideas for playground activities to start you off.

Catch the moment

You need to spend time teaching a child with ASD how to recognise feelings and emotions in themselves and others. The most effective way to do this is to *catch the moment* when the child is clearly emotional and then interpret this for them, linking cause and effect. For example: 'Jordan was working. Ross took her pens. Jordan is unhappy.' Later, you can use this kind of approach to talk about how a child *would* feel if such-and-such happened. You should also try to *catch the moment* when a child is behaving very appropriately and socially, using specific praise, for example: 'Thank you for *sharing*, Khalid.'

Circle of friends

This is a special kind of circle time directed at a child who finds it hard to make friends. It is a means of building up support networks for a child and, though not designed with ASD in mind, is being used increasingly for these pupils.

Circle time

The process of *circle time* involves key skills required of any individual belonging to a social group: awareness (knowing who I am), mastery (knowing what I can do) and social interaction (knowing how I function in the world of others). You can also use circles to deliver the National Curriculum when you are working in groups.

Game plan

For KS1 children at an early stage of social communication, try this approach. Spend ten minutes a session working or playing alongside them with another of the same toy or piece of equipment. Copy what they are doing. When they begin to notice what you are doing, move in to work or play with them, sharing the same object. Again, copy their actions. The idea is to encourage them to see that *their* behaviour is resulting in *your* behaviour. You can then begin to play turn-taking games, such as setting up and knocking down skittles.

Interpretation

Sometimes children with ASD give out negative social signals to other children without meaning to, and this can add to their isolation. Use your knowledge of the child and how they behave to interpret their behaviour to other children when necessary, for

example: 'George didn't mean to push you – that's his way of telling you that he would love to play a game with you' or 'Sara didn't mean to scream at you – she hasn't learned how to tell you that she is very busy and can't be disturbed at the moment. In time, she might be able to tell you in words.'

Mind mapping

Mind maps are very important techniques for improving the way children take notes. By using mind maps, you show the structure of the subject and linkages between points, as well as the raw facts contained in normal notes. Mind maps hold information in a format that the mind finds easy to remember and quick to review.

Use structure

Children with ASD can find it hard to cope with free play or open learning situations. When there is no clear structure, they might begin to behave inappropriately or retreat into repetitive or rigid behaviours. If you can be aware of this, it is helpful if you can introduce some structure even to free times. Offer clear choices of what to do next.

Working with challenges

ABC behaviour plan

It is essential that you make plans for changing any anti-social behaviour, for the sake of the other children as well as the child with ASD. Once you have carried out an ABC analysis of inappropriate behaviour (see pages 27 and 28), select just one area to work on first. This should be a behaviour that is fairly easy to change or one that is causing the biggest barrier to progress. Decide on a hypothesis as to what *you* think is keeping that behaviour going, based on your understanding of ASD. This will give you the opportunity to devise a plan for intervention, which you can then evaluate and redesign if you seem to be on the wrong track.

Broken record

Try not to elaborate and explain more and more each time a child with ASD does not comply with a direct request. This is likely to overload them with words. Instead, simply repeat the same instruction over and over, if necessary showing the child what to do as well as telling them. This is known as the *broken record* technique. Keep language short and simple, emphasising key words. Older pupils in class can also be helped to use this approach with a child who has ASD rather than escalating an argument. For example, you could teach children to repeat calmly, 'Alasdair, don't push me, please', rather than shouting or pushing Alasdair back.

Avoiding situations

When you carry out an ABC observation (see page 27), it may become obvious to you that you could alleviate a particular problem significantly by avoiding certain situations. For example, you could arrange for the child to miss assembly for a while, give the child a

responsibility to do during breaktime or place the child with a different peer group. Do not feel defeated that you are 'resorting' to avoidance strategies as they could be a sensible way of 'breaking the cycle' of the challenging behaviour and beginning to work on it step by step as part of a wider plan towards including the child.

Removing distractions

You may find it easiest to work with just one item or activity at a time, putting all other materials well out of sight. Try to reduce the number of options available, such as starting to complete a number puzzle with just the last three pieces of information missing. In order to give a non-verbal child the idea that they can have *choice*, show two activities or toys and ask the child to touch the one to be played with next.

Safe base

Provide a quiet 'safe base' where children can go if they are feeling overloaded or stressed. Children with ASD quickly feel stressed and anxious if there are many people about or if the demands on them are too great. If there is too much stimulation of any kind, they might revert to repetitive behaviours just to make the world predictable again. Once you have got to know the child, you will be able to see when the child is feeling stressed and let them move to the quiet area to 'wind down'. It is also important at some stage of the child's day for them to have time to be alone and to engage in a preferred activity of their own choosing. This approach helps to keep everyone in the class feeling calmer.

Warnings

Children with ASD find it hard to switch quickly into someone else's agenda. Give a warning before a change in activity (for example, 'It will be break in five minutes so finish off now'). If the child has little concept of the passage of time, use an egg-timer to signal the amount remaining. Egg-timers can also be used to encourage fair turn taking at the computer. Use *visual timetables* to help the child see what will happen next once they have finished what they are doing now.

My progress

My name: _____

My class: _____

I am trying to improve my social skills in these ways:

1. _____

2. _____

3. _____

I will have: 3 points if I did really well

                2 points if I did quite well

                1 point if I tried but didn't manage

If I collect _____ points in a week, this will happen:

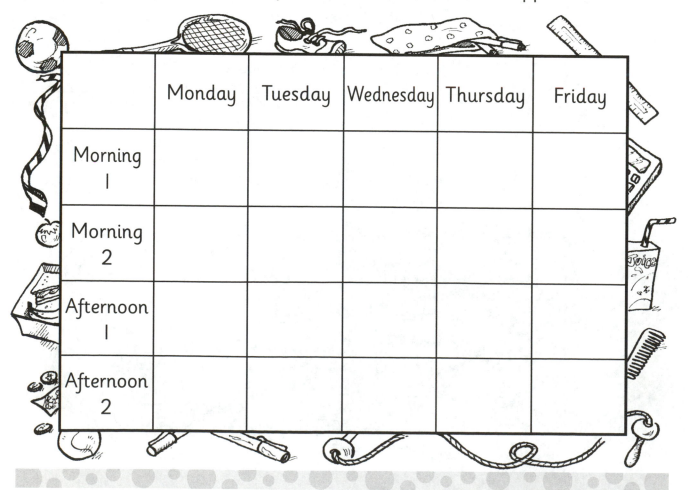

	Monday	Tuesday	Wednesday	Thursday	Friday
Morning 1					
Morning 2					
Afternoon 1					
Afternoon 2					

SPECIAL NEEDS **in the primary years:** Autistic Spectrum Difficulties

SPEAKING AND LISTENING

This strand of the National Curriculum is usually very challenging for pupils with ASD since they often lack the intrinsic enjoyment of communicating. In fact, they might see very little point in it at all and your task becomes one of giving them a reason to communicate and something to communicate about. Throughout these activity chapters you will find that words in italic can be cross-referenced to Chapters 1 and 3 so that they serve as a shorthand for the explanations you met earlier in the book.

Many children with ASD (and particularly those with Asperger's syndrome) will develop expressive language reasonably well but tend to use it rather woodenly, pedantically and without flexibility. There is also a very literal use and understanding of language, so that turns of phrase, irony or double meaning need full explanation. You need to 'stay one step ahead' on any texts that you use in order to *avoid ambiguity* and be conscious of any passages that might need particular explanation or a concrete example.

Listening skills will probably need teaching at first, perhaps by using structured games to *teach communication skills* at *circle time* or through *musical interactions*. You will probably find that your best chance of teaching and learning will come as opportunities arise throughout the school day as you *encourage communication*, use *careful questioning* and *catch the moment*. You might find that *turn taking* in conversations again needs to be taught directly by planning activities that introduce reciprocal interaction through *game plans* or *musical interactions*.

In order to support the children as they communicate together, you may need to use your own knowledge of the child and use *interpretation* so that other children can begin to see how the child's behaviour can also communicate intent. *A communication book* can make this easier for everyone if the child is still at an early stage of communicating.

When it has developed, language itself can become a useful vehicle for teaching and supporting the child with ASD. Spoken instructions can be reinforced with visual prompts in order to give the child *clear expectations* of what will happen next and to provide them with *warnings* of changes in routines. *Developing scripts* and social stories can be an excellent way to help children with ASD cope more flexibly with new situations.

When planning a speaking and listening activity for the whole group, you might need to provide children with ASD with a clear place to sit (marking it with a chair or cushion) and make plans to include them in the group step-by-small-step. Group times can be very stressful and some children with ASD will cope with either being part of the group or in following what is said, though not both together. So, much of your planning for children with ASD is a matter of finding balances and gradually encouraging greater flexibility.

AGE RANGE
Five to seven.

GROUP SIZE
Small group.

LEARNING OBJECTIVE FOR ALL THE CHILDREN
● To use language and actions to explore and convey situations, characters and emotions.

INDIVIDUAL LEARNING TARGET
● To listen and then carry out a simple action.

Talking hands

Children with ASD need to learn listening skills early on. The use of a musical *circle time* can be an excellent way of helping them focus and yet remain relaxed.

What you need
Drum and some other non-pitched percussion instruments (for example: rattles, shakers and triangles).

Preparation
Start with the warm-up chant described in teaching communication skills on page 39. Then practise being able to say nice things in a cross voice and harsh and angry things in a soft voice. Collect instruments and have them ready for the activity.

What to do
Start the activity by talking about how we communicate. Pretend to pat a dog and talk to it in a soothing way but then, keeping the tone the same, scold it for making a puddle on the carpet. Finally, change to a 'telling off' tone of voice and say really kind things. Ask the children how they think the dog felt. Hopefully, someone will volunteer that the way we say things affects how it is understood.

Using the drum, play a soft, slow rhythmical beat and ask the children how they feel (for example: calm, sleepy and relaxed). Play a light, quick beat and ask the same question. Ask for volunteers to try to create a feeling with a musical instrument.

Pick two children to come to the centre of the circle to play the instruments. Tell them that they are going to have a conversation without speaking! Say to one of them: 'Pretend you are (insert the name of a teacher in the school) and you have just found out that (insert the other child's name) has left the tap on in the toilets and that the water is running down the stairs,' or some other similar scenario. Ask that child to play their instrument in the way that the teacher might feel – perhaps loudly and in a cross manner. Ask the other child to play theirs as they might feel – perhaps rather timidly.

The other children follow the 'conversation' by watching, listening and trying to name some of the feelings being acted out.

Special support
At first, you will need to keep this simple for a child with ASD. Start with a session with a *key worker*, showing the child how to make angry, happy, scary, sad or sleepy sounds on a drum. Then help the child generalise these new skills into the group activity.

Extension
Make up a sound story with instruments, playing them in different ways to convey strong feelings, such as a scary walk in the jungle – but with a happy ending!

AGE RANGE
Five to seven.

GROUP SIZE
Whole group.

LEARNING OBJECTIVE FOR ALL THE CHILDREN
● To take turns in speaking.

INDIVIDUAL LEARNING TARGET
● To respond to a simple spoken instruction given to the group.

Oh no, it's not!

Children with ASD can be helped to speak and listen if they can learn that language has its own routines and rules. This simple activity uses repetition and sentence completion to make it predictable and 'safe'.

What you need
List of closed questions or statements that allow either a 'yes' or 'no' answer (linked to topic work or general awareness); three soft toys (for example: Sammy Snake, Penny Panda and Lenny Lion).

Preparation
Make sure that the children know how to take turns when speaking and can also speak in chorus.

What to do
Divide the class in two. One group is the 'Oh yes, it is' group and the other is the 'Oh no, it's not' group. Let them practise their line a few times, in chorus and alternately, like a pantomime audience. Pick a child from one group (if there is an odd number of children, pick a child from the larger group). This child stands at the front with Sammy Snake. Give the first child in each group another soft toy.

Stand at the back and make a statement such as, 'It is raining today.' The child at the front makes Sammy Snake say, 'It's raining today.' The child in the 'Yes' group who has Penny Panda stands up and makes Penny Panda say, 'Yes, it is raining today.' The child then passes Penny Panda to the next child in the 'Yes' group. Then the child with Lenny Lion stands up and makes Lenny say, 'No, it's not raining today', and then passes Lenny Lion to the next child. The child with Sammy Snake chooses which statement is correct and changes place with the child who said it, giving them Sammy Snake. That child then comes and stands at the front of the classroom. You make another statement and the process starts again.

You can control the pace of the activity and also which child stands at the front by your use of statements. The soft toys are not strictly necessary, but they add a certain anonymity and make it easier for children to make statements that they know are not true. The activity encourages good listening, speaking and memory skills and teaches turn taking.

Special support
If this is too complex for a child with ASD at first, ask that child to be your helper at the back. Once the other children have taken their turn, ask your helper a direct question, such as: 'Is it raining today?' and encourage a yes or no response.

Extension
Ask the children to prepare their own statements and observations.

AGE RANGE
Seven to nine.

GROUP SIZE
Small group.

LEARNING OBJECTIVE FOR ALL THE CHILDREN
To combine understanding of emotional vocabulary with facial and body language.

INDIVIDUAL LEARNING TARGET
To indicate which of two puppets is happy, lonely, puzzled, and so on.

Making faces

Children who find it hard to grasp abstract concepts are particularly challenged by abstract description words. This activity aims to help the child with ASD develop their vocabulary.

Preparation
Find two puppets that have facial features you can alter. Otherwise make two sock puppets. Their expressions can be easily manipulated provided you have practised talking to them! Prepare some 'emotions cards' containing single words that describe someone's thoughts, feelings or state of mind – for example: greedy, hurt, annoyed, excited, proud, worried. The 'Free sweets' story on photocopiable page 52 contains other similar words. Practise telling the 'Free sweets' story using the two puppets.

What to do
This activity helps children to understand the use of body language in conveying feelings. Children with ASD need explicit teaching of this important skill. Tell the children the 'Free sweets' story using the two puppets. Use the questions provided at the end of each scene to prompt the children to think about the sort of feelings each of the puppets might have had. How can they tell? Take them through the use of words, facial expressions and body language, as well as the context of the story.

Now choose one of the emotions cards. Show two of the children how to mime the emotion that is on the card and present it to the class. Ask the class to guess what the emotion being mimed was. Do this again with several other examples, so that the children understand what is expected of them.

Give out the emotion cards, one to each child. In groups of no more than three, ask them to prepare a short mime in which they must present the emotion through facial expression or body language. They might want to think up a situation where these emotions might be expressed and act this out. After each group has performed their mime, let the children guess the words. What was it that helped them to understand the emotion?

Special support
Children with ASD need explicit teaching about the use of body language in conveying feelings. If necessary, introduce the skill one to one with a *key worker* before working in a group. *Catch the moment* to praise the child for using these skills in everyday situations as this is a very helpful way to *teach communication skills* to them.

Extension
Use this activity to introduce other abstract words. You can also use drama scripts to introduce similes and metaphors.

AGE RANGE
Seven to nine.

GROUP SIZE
Whole group, then pairs.

LEARNING OBJECTIVE FOR ALL THE CHILDREN
● To be able to form questions and statements.

INDIVIDUAL LEARNING TARGET
● To join in a simple sentence-completion game.

What is he doing?

He is . . .

Question or statement?

Children with ASD are easily confused by questions. Here is an exercise which uses a speaking and listening activity to encourage children to complete spoken statements instead.

What you need
'Stick figures' and a set of question words (what, why, when, how, and so on) on an overhead projector; copies of question and statement beginnings (see 'Preparation' below).

Preparation
Clip Art of 'stick figures' can easily be accessed from internet-based applications, such as Microsoft Design Gallery. Choose a selection of images of figures engaged in different activities, such as walking, running, talking and sleeping. Prepare one set of question words for the OHP. Make enough copies for all the children of question and statement beginnings, such as: 'Where do you go…?' 'I go…' 'What is your favourite…?' 'My favourite… is…'

What to do
Begin the activity by showing one of the stick figures on the overhead projector along with the set of question words. Ask the children to form a sentence about the stick figure, beginning with one of the words displayed. After each question, ask a child to give a possible reply, for example: 'What is he doing?', 'He is running.' 'How long will he run for?', 'He will run for an hour.' Once the children have got used to this, explain that one of these is a question and the other a statement about the stick figure. Continue with some of the other stick figures.

Give each of the children a copy of the question and statement beginnings. Tell the class that they are now going to interview you. They may ask you questions, using and completing the question beginnings on the sheet, and you will reply, giving a statement. Sometimes you will not finish a statement, but will ask them to guess what you are going to say.

Finally, put the children in pairs so that one child asks a question, using one of the beginnings, and the other child replies, using the beginning of the statement and then completing it. The children could perform their best question and statement to the class, perhaps leaving out the final part of the statement for the others to guess.

Special support
Make use of *careful questioning* to teach the child with ASD how question sentences work.

Extension
The children can form their own question and statement beginnings.

AGE RANGE
Nine to eleven.

GROUP SIZE
Whole class split into groups of two to four children.

LEARNING OBJECTIVE FOR ALL THE CHILDREN
● To realise what another person might be thinking or feeling.

INDIVIDUAL LEARNING TARGET
● To practise making a difficult request.

Think before you speak

Speaking and listening time can provide excellent opportunities for discussing social situations and providing children with ASD with new options for behaving. This activity uses talk and role play.

What you need
Situation cards, one set per group (see photocopiable pages 53 and 54); large thought bubbles copied on to paper (or drawn on the board); individual whiteboards and whiteboard pens, one per child.

Preparation
Prepare some large thought bubbles (and laminate if possible) – 'Autoshapes' on Microsoft Word includes a template that can be used for this purpose. This activity works best when the class is set up in a horseshoe formation.

What to do
Tell the children that they are going to perform short role plays about difficult situations. They will need to show what a character is thinking as well as what they are saying.

Using one of the situation cards, set up a freeze frame, for example: a child going to the headteacher to say they are sorry for breaking a window. Have one child as the headteacher and another as the window breaker. Ask two children to stand behind them holding thought bubbles.

Using 'forum theatre' (see the *National Literacy Strategy Speaking, Listening, Learning* for more information), ask the remainder of the children what the two characters might be thinking. Let the children with the thought bubbles write down some of these ideas. From these thoughts, establish with the children what words are likely to be spoken by the characters. Let the actors choose which words to say.

Give out the different situations to the groups of children. Let them discuss what thoughts each person might have, write these on their bubbles, then discuss what words are going to be said and decide who will say them. The children then perform their role plays to the class. After each performance, discuss with the whole class if there were any other things that might have been thought or said.

Special support
Children with ASD will need a high level of support if they are to be able to ascribe thoughts and feelings to others. Start this activity with a *key worker* and then help the child participate in the group, giving feedback and using *interpretation* to aid understanding.

Extension
Help the children imagine and perform their own situations. Use this to explore ways of behaving and reacting in a range of situations.

Babble gabble

Children with ASD can be helped to think more sequentially and flexibly by considering choices. This is always easiest to do when there is a visual prompt.

AGE RANGE
Nine to eleven.

GROUP SIZE
Whole class split into groups of two to three children.

LEARNING OBJECTIVE FOR ALL THE CHILDREN
● To be able to retell a story in order and to choose an appropriate ending.

INDIVIDUAL LEARNING TARGET
● To choose an appropriate ending for a story.

What you need
Copy of the 'Babble gabble' story on photocopiable page 54.

Preparation
If possible, practise the story so that you know it well enough to tell rather than read it.

What to do
Tell the children the story. Let them know beforehand that they are going to have to retell the story and so they will need to listen carefully. For some groups you may need to tell the story twice or go through the basic structure of what happened again before they start the exercise.

Number the children in each pair or group (one to three). Ask the children to tell the story to each other, putting in as much detail as they can remember. Number one will start off while the others listen. On the shout of 'change', number two must take over. Change over as often as you want. If any storyteller gets stuck, or relates the story in the wrong order, the other children in the group can help. The CRAARK! at the end will tell you when some have finished. Any early finishers should start again, with child number two beginning. Any pairs too far behind the rest can be told to 'gabble' the rest of the story in one minute.

At the end of the lesson, ask the children what is missing from the story (the ending). Ask them to predict what the ending will be. Pick the suggestion the children like the most and prepare a spoken story ending together.

Special support
Draw four pictures of possible endings with text beneath and ask the child with ASD to consider each one. Which is best? What would they need to describe as a storyteller? What would the characters be saying or doing? If necessary, make up a simpler version of the story.

Extension
Some children may wish to write up their story ending. They could also work in pairs, one child starting a written story and another completing it.

Free sweets

Scene 1

Nico and Sam often go to the park. Nico has loads of friends and is **happy,** having plenty of games to play. Sam cannot seem to make friends and is often **lonely.**
Look at the two puppets. Can you guess which puppet is which? How can you tell?

Scene 2

It hasn't always been this way. One of the puppets used to give out lots of sweets to his friends, which made him very popular. In fact he would **boast** about how many friends he had and **make fun** of the other puppet, who had none. The other puppet was **puzzled** by how sweets could make you popular.
Look at the expressions Nico and Sam now have. Which one is boastful and popular? How can you tell? Which is puzzled? How do you know?

Scene 3

The puppet was so puzzled that he decided to follow the other to the park. On the way was a newsagent's shop. It was a Thursday. Pocket-money day was not until Friday and therefore no puppet ever had any money left. And yet the puppet came out with stacks of sweets looking very **shifty and guilty**. The first puppet realised what was happening and was **determined** to tell the truth.
What do you think was happening? Who was shifty and guilty? Who was determined?

Scene 4

By the time the sweets arrived at the park, the truth had been told. The so-called friends refused to take them as they were stolen. This left one puppet very **lonely and disgraced** while the other had loads of friends because he could be **trusted.** *How have they ended up? Why is Sam lonely? Why is Nico happy?*

Situations

Your mum has spent ages making a meal that you do not like.

You do not want a classmate to join in a game, as last time she ruined it.

You want to ask your dad to let you sleep over at a friend's house, but know that it is your sister's birthday party that same evening.

You have to ask your teacher to allow you not to do PE because you have forgotten your PE kit.

You are meeting your best friend for the first time since they reported you for kicking someone under the table.

Your parents are taking the family out for a meal at a restaurant. You prefer to go for a burger. 	Your brother or sister has been on the computer for ages and you want to have a go. 
You need to go and see the headteacher to explain how you broke the window at breaktime.	You want to play and be friends with someone else in class but, last time you asked, they said that they were not interested.

Babble gabble story

*L*ong ago, in the mists of time lay a forgotten wood. Within the wood a forgotten hill. Upon the hill a forgotten castle.

The castle stood as dark as sin, as still as bone, until... Gawain came. A shining knight, brave and fearless, upon his white horse, Giselde.

Now Giselde could smell evil, and within that wood, upon that hill, she whinnied – neeeeeiiiigh to her master not to enter the castle.

Gawain, killer of dragons, of monsters, of snakes, laughed at his horse, "Ha, ha, Giselde. Have you forgotten? I am Gawain and fearless is my name!"

Tying Giselde to a crooked yew tree, Gawain approached the gate to the castle. BOOM! BOOM! BOOM! His chainmailed fists struck the gate.

The gate swung wide with an eerie creak – eeech! No one had opened it! Sunlight flickered on the dusty, cobwebbed, oaken tables before him. A feast was laid out upon it. Steaming turkeys, dripping roasted pig, but no guests. His stomach rumbled – Blup, blup blup! – for it was three days since he had eaten.

A candle burned next to one place. Reluctantly, he moved towards it. As he did so, the chair pulled back on its own and invited him to sit at the feast. It was then that he heard above him a loud, crow-like CRAARK!

WRITING

Children with ASD can sometimes have difficulties with spelling and writing and this can be part of a more general difficulty in organisation, motor coordination and flexible thinking. It can be hard for them to organise their thoughts into sequences ready for writing down. They often fail to provide an adequate context for the reader and report too briefly or incompletely. Sometimes sentence construction is lacking and a list of facts is produced instead. You can build on this tendency by actually encouraging note taking and the use of bullet points and then using these as starting points to 'pad out' the text and encourage fuller sentences around each item. Another excellent way in is to encourage the making of *mind maps*, again helping the child fill these out with sentences as a separate exercise from hatching the ideas. The best advice, at least initially, is to help the children break down the learning tasks into steps and to direct them at each stage.

Sometimes children with ASD have physical difficulties in actually manipulating their writing implement and you can experiment with different types of pen and grip in order to give them better control. Children with ASD can be very specific in their preferences and you might find that one kind of pen or writing paper works 'like magic' compared to another! You may find it helpful to ask the child to dictate ideas on to a tape recorder or even via voice recognition software on to a computer. Some children with ASD have found it much easier to word-process than to write by hand, and the way that the computer works actually helps them to slow down and sequence their ideas. When recording actual experiences or outings, a series of digital photographs can provide helpful visual prompts for generating the writing.

The Literacy Hour can be used productively for pupils with ASD by making the best use of visual images, texts and props. Steady the pace if you can and *structure* the written part carefully, providing extra support to help the child organise ideas before writing. Allow withdrawal to the *safe base* if a large group or fast pace creates overload for the child. Return after a while to re-focus the child, *engaging attention* and setting *clear expectations* and directions. Make use of the *finish box*, so that the child knows what to do at the end of the writing activity, and use the *visual timetable* to sandwich a stress-free activity with more demanding learning tasks.

AGE RANGE
Five to seven.

GROUP SIZE
Small group.

LEARNING OBJECTIVE FOR ALL THE CHILDREN
● To develop a fluent cursive movement for writing.

INDIVIDUAL LEARNING TARGET
● To hold and use a writing implement with control.

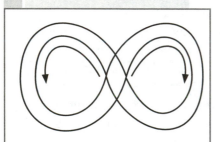

Racetracks

Children with ASD sometimes have mild clumsiness that makes it hard for them to control a pencil. In this activity, children experiment with different writing implements and media to find their best combination for early writing.

What you need
A 'racetrack' sheet for each child (see diagram, below); selection of different coloured pens and pencils, (more than one per child); a seconds timer.

Preparation
On a sheet of A4 paper, draw two large circles which touch. Draw an inner circle half a centimetre away from the original line to create a track. Photocopy enough copies for all the children.

What to do
Present the sheet in landscape orientation and explain that it represents a racetrack. Talk about what you may find on a racetrack or next to a racetrack. The children can draw in the centre of the circles and around the edges to make the racetrack more realistic, if appropriate.

Explain that, on a racetrack, it is important that everyone travels in the same direction. On this racetrack they must follow a specific route (see diagram, left). This is important as it mirrors the correct direction for forming letters. Choose a starting point and encourage the children to 'walk the route' with the first finger of their writing hand. The child can then choose a pen or pencil.

Explain that the children are going to see how fast and how smoothly each pen or pencil can travel. They must pull it and not push (important for ink pens and good handwriting technique) and try to stay on the 'track'.

Set the timer for an appropriate time (start with five seconds) and challenge the children to trace the path of the racetrack as many times as they can, counting the 'laps' as they go. Repeat with other colours, pens and pencils, and sheets, as appropriate.

Special support
Teach this movement by tracing a figure of eight in the air, using a hand-over-hand technique, to encourage the correct arm movement, if the child will let you. *Keep it concrete* by encouraging the child to follow the movement with toy cars on one of the racetrack sheets.

Extension
Move on to practising the pencil movements involved in the letters 'o', 'a', 'c' and 'e', covering sheets of paper with differently coloured letters.

Sentence envelopes

Children with ASD might see little point in writing sentences. This is an activity that makes sentence construction fun for everyone.

AGE RANGE
Five to seven.

GROUP SIZE
Individually or in small groups.

LEARNING OBJECTIVE FOR ALL THE CHILDREN
● To write familiar words and attempt unfamiliar ones.

INDIVIDUAL LEARNING TARGET
● To write one sentence independently.

What you need
Sentence envelopes (described below), at least one per child.

Preparation
Type or print clearly a sentence on the front of each self-seal, DL-sized envelope. Place the words of the sentence on separate cards inside the envelope. Then handwrite the sentence under the bottom self-seal flap as model handwriting (hint: a little talcum powder on the flaps will stop the envelope sealing by accident). The sentences should target the children's interests as well as their reading and spelling ability.

What to do
This can be an independent exercise or supported by an assistant. Ask each child to read the front of the envelope, then, with eyes shut, say the sentence. As soon as the sentence can be repeated accurately, spread the word cards on the table. Let the child put the word cards in the correct order for the sentence, using clues such as capital letters and full stops.

Place the cards back in the envelope and ask each child to write their sentence. By looking at the model handwriting under the flap, the children can then check their performance. Prepare more envelopes than required and give the extras to early finishers.

If used in the Literacy Hour with children of similar ability, the sentence envelopes can be numbered so that they build into a story or poem. Using this format, each child will need a numbered sheet with space to write each sentence, so that they do not all have to start with the first sentence. This activity encourages awareness of story structure as well as sharing and a sense of 'taking part', which may not be familiar to a child with ASD.

Special support
Tune in to language levels and use strong *motivators* by starting with a sentence that the child has made up, centering around a particular interest.

Extension
There is plenty of scope for differentiation, for example: the number of words per sentence and the difficulty of vocabulary. In addition, the content of the sentence can be targeted for specific children or used to suggest sentences which can be employed later in subject areas.

AGE RANGE
Seven to nine.

GROUP SIZE
Whole group, then pairs.

LEARNING OBJECTIVE FOR ALL THE CHILDREN
● To organise and develop different aspects of a character using a mind map.

INDIVIDUAL LEARNING TARGET
● To make a simple mind map and build prose from it.

Mind the map

It can be hard for a child with ASD to organise their thoughts sufficiently to put them on paper. This activity uses simple *mind mapping* to plan and then record a piece of written work.

What you need
Character descriptions; pictures of faces; class list of adjectives; access to computers, one per pair; mind mapping software such as MindManager® Pro (optional).

Preparation
Prepare three or four character descriptions from children's books. Summarise information about their appearances, personality and background. Photocopy these descriptions, as well as any pictures of interesting faces, to prompt the children's imagination. Have available a class list of adjectives that describe characters' features and personality and discuss these adjectives before the lesson.

What to do
Together read some of the character descriptions. Discuss the features of each character, which characters the children like and what they like about them. Pick out the different aspects of any character that a narrator would need to describe and make a class list (these will form the branches of the mind map). Tell the children that they are now going to make up their own character.

Model how to add branches to their mind maps for different character features, for example: face, clothing, personality, mannerisms, background, sayings (see diagram, left). Take one of the branches and add subheadings, for example: eyes, chin, moustache, hair, nose. Add a sentence to one of the subheadings, using the adjective list from an earlier lesson, for example: 'His black eyes stabbed into everyone he saw'. Explain how the use of the mind map helps to order the children's character descriptions.

Let the children work in pairs to produce their own mind maps, perhaps using computer software.

Special support
Set *clear expectations* to keep the child on task and *give feedback* regularly. If the child becomes distracted, use the *broken record* technique to return them to task. If the child has very literal understanding, take time to explain what figurative speech is.

Extension
Help the children look at the link phrases between each sentence so that they tie together. Children could draw their character and present them in a display.

	crystal blue	
	slanted	
	staring	
	eyes	
evil	chin	clothing
good	eyebrows	height
plotting	nose	unusual features -scar
	hair	
Thoughts	**Face**	**Physical**

Character - Lascar

Movements	**Personality**
mannerisms	weaknesses
habits	strengths
quickness	likes/dislikes
	Subtopic

AGE RANGE
Seven to nine.

GROUP SIZE
Whole group.

LEARNING OBJECTIVE FOR ALL THE CHILDREN
● To write an informal and formal letter with a purpose.

INDIVIDUAL LEARNING TARGET
● To write a short letter.

Get a response

Children with ASD need to see a point to writing. In this activity, letter writing is used in connection with their topic of particular interest.

What you need
Selection of formal and informal letters – see *Children's Letters* by Julie Garnett (Longman) for examples; addresses of various embassies; supply of paper; envelopes; stamps; a pen for each child.

Preparation
Write a list of features of formal and informal letters on the board. The children will need the address of a relative they are going to write to. You can obtain embassy addresses from a London telephone directory or from an internet directory.

What to do
This activity can be completed over a series of lessons. Tell the children that they are going to write two different types of letters: one to a relative and the other to an embassy. Say that the letters will be posted and hopefully they will receive some responses.

Explain that their first letter will be informal and to a relative that they do not see every day. Show an example of a letter to a relative. Discuss its informal, chatty style and content. How will the children end the letter? Ask the class to suggest an outline for each paragraph and put a list of features on the board. Let the children draft their letters independently. Then put the children in pairs and get them to swap letters, so that the partner can check the other's letter for content and sense against the class list. Then send off the letters!

For the second letter, ask the children to think of a country that they would like to find out about. Tell them about the role of embassies. Discuss the layout and style of a formal letter. Talk about the need for an introduction and paragraphs to demonstrate what they know about the country and what questions they would like answered. Ask the children to write a formal letter to an embassy, requesting information about the country they represent.

Follow the drafting and proofreading work outlined above and send off the letters. When the responses arrive, some children might wish to read them to the class and then write a reply.

Special support
Talk to the chosen relative ahead of time, so that you can *encourage communication* from someone who will write back regularly! *Use structure* for letter writing and consider a *taped text* in which you record the rules.

Extension
Encourage the children to begin writing their own letters, for example to pen pals, clubs, fanzines, and so on.

AGE RANGE
Nine to eleven.

GROUP SIZE
Whole group.

LEARNING OBJECTIVE FOR ALL THE CHILDREN
● To develop the use of props to create interesting plot lines and help structure formal reports.

INDIVIDUAL LEARNING TARGET
● To record the key points of a lesson.

Police report

Visual props can be very helpful for children with ASD when they have to remember and record a story. In this activity, the props make the lesson memorable for everyone.

What you need

Chalk or masking tape; clipboards and pens; access to the playground or hall; various props, for example: key, ticket, cryptic note, photograph, an odd shaped stone (any small item that might have a 'story' behind it); the report on photocopiable page 62.

Preparation

Mark out a dead body outline either in chalk on the playground or using masking tape in the hall. Place the various props around it. Make copies of the report on photocopiable page 62, one per child.

What to do

Tell the children that they are detectives and that they have been called to the scene of a possible crime. Show them the outline of the body and the items found around it.

The children's role in the investigation is to find out all they can about the items and submit a report about them to the court.

Put the children in groups of four to six. Let the children examine the items by giving them out, one to each group. Let them discuss the object and then pass it on to the next group. Then, as a class, discuss what the children have found and what they could deduce from each item. Tell the children that they may need to use their imaginations to add depth to their report.

Back in the classroom, look at the beginning of the formal report with the children. Discuss the style and language that is used. Note that the key has been investigated and found to be very important. Ask the children to continue, writing separate paragraphs for each of the other items.

Special support

To avoid children becoming fixated on this activity, use a *finish box* to 'put the story to bed'. Support the child's understanding by pointing out *good role models* and ideas. Encourage them to think more flexibly by helping them make links between the objects and their possible meanings.

Extension

Ask the children to continue using this stimulus to write a murder mystery story.

AGE RANGE
Nine to eleven.

GROUP SIZE
Any.

LEARNING OBJECTIVE FOR ALL THE CHILDREN

● To understand what an idiom is and to know its real meaning.

INDIVIDUAL LEARNING TARGET

● To understand the double meanings in a series of jokes.

Idiotic idioms

Children who find it hard to understand abstract concepts find subtleties in language difficult to grasp. In this activity, humour and writing combine to encourage flexibility of thought for the child with ASD.

What you need
Dictionary of idioms, for example: *Fun with English – Idioms* by George Beal (Kingfisher); copied sheet of idioms; websites with idioms; blank A4 paper folded in half; colouring materials.

Preparation
Put together a list of idioms with space beside each one for the children to write down its meaning. Examples of idioms might include: 'It is raining cats and dogs' and 'He is green with envy'. Prepare an example layout of an 'idiom picture': draw the literal meaning on one side with no text. On the other side will be the idiom with its real meaning, both written and in picture form.

What to do
Take a couple of idioms that you feel would appeal to your group. 'Ham up' a scene in which it was actually raining cats and dogs, for example, either by yourself or with a few children.

Explain that idioms are ways of saying something particular to a culture. Talk about why idioms are used (they exaggerate by comparison facts or feelings, often using humour for impact). What problems would people from other countries have in understanding them? Tell the children that they are going to provide pictures to help others understand what the idiom really means. Give out your prepared sheets of idioms. In pairs, let the children discuss the literal and then the real meaning of the idioms. If they have difficulties, they can look the idioms up in a dictionary or on a website. Show them the example of an 'idiom picture'. Say that these will form a display for people to guess which idiom it is they have drawn. Give the children time to complete an 'idiom picture' for the display.

Eyes Are Too big for your Belly.

Special support
Many children with Asperger's syndrome love this activity. *Encourage communication* by helping the child produce their own dictionary of sayings to take through school and use when the time is right!

Extension
Children can continue collecting idioms and place them on a large sheet on the display board.

Report

STATEMENT OF witness
S9 Criminal Justice Act 1967

I, Detective Constable _____ make this statement knowing that if anything I say is untrue then I may be prosecuted.

Signed _____

On the 12th Day of May 2005 I attended Byways Park, Elton at 9.10am. There I saw an outline of a body that had been removed for examination by forensic scientists. Left on the ground were several items. I was detailed by DI Grief to find out as much as I could about these items. My investigations revealed the following information.

I took the key to Mister Minit on Main Street, Elton. I was informed that the key was unusual and would not fit a normal house lock or padlock. I was referred to SafeKeys of Barnsley. I travelled to Barnsley the following day, the 13th May. SafeKeys informed me that they did make that particular key. It was used to fit special chamber locks on bank safes. However, upon testing it, they informed me that it was a fake as it did not have the correct number upon it. It was likely to fit the safe at Elton Bank. I travelled back to Elton that same day and in the presence of Mr Nick Cash, the bank manager, I found that it did indeed open that safe.

The train ticket . . .

NUMBER AND ALGEBRA

Number can be a real strength for many children with ASD since they might have an intrinsic interest in numbers and calculating. Your role becomes one of making the interest appropriate and meaningful so that it develops from simply 'collecting' numbers and performing mathematical 'tricks' to a useful and productive life skill. As with other strands of the curriculum, start with the strengths (the child's interest in number) and use these to support the areas of weakness (understanding instructions and handling abstract concepts).

Many children with ASD have difficulty understanding complex instructions in numberwork and algebra. Simplify your language and give instructions one step at a time, showing the child what to do and working through examples to 'get them going'. Try to stay with one particular mathematical rule and process for a while, rather than dotting around from one to another – this might involve you filleting different maths schemes or individually designing tasks to consolidate that rule or process. Teaching mathematics to a child with ASD can be a real test of your skill as a teacher. There is logic, routine and precision involved and this will appeal to the child with ASD – your task is to make the rules and processes as clear as crystal to the pupil. In order to support generalisation and practical application of what you are teaching, use objects and pictures to aid the child's understanding.

Some children with ASD are so fascinated by numbers that they ask the same question repeatedly, interrupting the lesson. Set a clear rule for the class, restricting interruptions to three, and then set up a separate time to go through the child's question. Praise non-interruption. Also, these children might have difficulties understanding the language of mathematics and become confused when different words are used to mean the same thing (add and sum, multiply and times, divide and share). Find practical examples to help the child make sense of these words, and make a collection of words on cards for the child to refer to. If the child cannot handle 'What?' questions, offer incomplete mathematical sentences instead for the child to complete.

Algebra will at first be baffling to a child with ASD since the symbols are used to stand for many different values. Once 'cracked', many children with ASD can find great academic pleasure in algebraic calculations, though might find it harder to use them to solve real mathematical problems. Again, your ingenuity in finding practical examples will be needed to support their 'real' understanding.

AGE RANGE
Five to seven.

GROUP SIZE
Any.

LEARNING OBJECTIVE FOR ALL THE CHILDREN
● To understand a general statement and investigate whether particular cases match it.

INDIVIDUAL LEARNING TARGET
● To use their interest in numbers appropriately in a learning situation.

I spy

Children with ASD can sometimes be fascinated by numbers. This activity supports early number work and helps them to excel in front of their peers.

What you need
Number frieze; drum.

Preparation
Place the number frieze high up so that the children will be able to see it.

What to do
Seat the children so that they are all able to see the number frieze. Introduce the activity with 'I spy' but, instead of 'beginning with' and a letter name, ask the children to spot simple objects, such as 'something on the windowsill' (a plant pot). Children with ASD often have difficulty responding quickly and so this provides a good warm-up exercise.

When ready, introduce something from the number frieze such as, 'I spy with my little eye some ducks. How many can you see?' (For example, your number frieze might have six ducks for number 6.) Select a child to respond, for example: 'Peter, how many ducks are there? Come and show us. Tap the drum that many times. I want the rest of you to watch and make sure he does it right.'

Peter taps the drum six times while the rest of the class count silently. They can then vote with a show of hands as to whether Peter was right. Then, select another number using only the picture that represents it on the number frieze and invite another child to tap the drum.

Special support
Children with ASD sometimes have difficulty with the concept of pictures and symbols representing concrete objects. This activity is a good way of introducing those concepts yet *keeping it concrete*. It is better not to pick the child with ASD for the first turn, as they are usually happier to have a role model to follow. Always *engage attention* by saying the child's name first so that they are ready to respond.

Extension
You can also just show a number on a card – being careful not to name it – to see if the visual stimulus is sufficient for understanding. There are endless adaptations to this activity, depending on whether a simple demonstration of the 'fourness' of four or the 'sixness' of six is required or more complex mathematical concepts are to be covered, such as simple addition or subtraction.

AGE RANGE
Five to seven.

GROUP SIZE
Four to six.

LEARNING OBJECTIVE FOR ALL THE CHILDREN
● To begin to understand addition as combining two groups of objects and subtraction as 'taking away'

INDIVIDUAL LEARNING TARGET
● To respond to 'add' and 'take away' using counting materials.

Chuffa chuffa

Children with ASD can find it hard to grasp the language of numberwork and need practical examples. Here is an activity to help.

What you need
Collection of Unifix cubes, enough so each child has ten; a 14cm diameter coloured circle for each child; a die and spinner marked with plus and minus signs (optional).

Preparation
Seat the children at equal intervals around a table and place a coloured circle in front of each of them. Place ten Unifix cubes on each circle.

What to do
Say to the children that the circles represent their stations and that they should choose one of the cubes to be the train driver. Each child must choose a different colour. Allow one circuit of the track – round the perimeter of the table. Each child drives their 'train' to the next station. Train noises can be made if appropriate.

Now, tell a number story about who gets on or off the train – with the children's help if possible. Getting on the train represents addition: 'How many people are on the train?' Getting off is subtraction: 'How many people are left on the train?' 'How many people are left on the station?'

The variations begin when you decide how many people get on or off the train. The fun can really start when three people get off and two people get on. Be careful, though, because some children might not agree with the same people getting off and straight back on again!

Use as much mathematical vocabulary as possible, such as: 'This is a four-cube train, add one more to make it five.' However, do be very careful to explain that 'take-away' in this context means someone getting off the train and not a ready-prepared meal! After each station stop, start the story again and ask the children to move to the next station in an anticlockwise direction.

Special support
If necessary, place the child with ASD in a smaller group of two or three that is supported by an adult. Use this as an opportunity to *teach turn taking* and to make use of *good role models*.

Extension
If you have a die and spinner, these can be used to decide how many passengers are added and taken away. Older children sometimes enjoy this element of chance, whereas the younger children often prefer the story element and do not realise how much they are learning.

AGE RANGE
Seven to nine.

GROUP SIZE
Any.

LEARNING OBJECTIVE FOR ALL THE CHILDREN
● To learn how to do linear addition based upon a practical example.

INDIVIDUAL LEARNING TARGET
● To turn a practical addition problem into a linear sum.

Shopaholics

Children with ASD might find it easy to handle familiarly presented 'sums' but much harder to solve practical problems. This activity aims to help children translate mathematical problems into written sums.

What you need
Range of boxes, plastic bottles and tubes, at least two per child; sticky labels; money or base ten equipment; calculators.

Preparation
Prior to the activity, ask the children to bring in any boxes, plastic bottles and tubes from home to form your collection. Create two shops in the classroom: for example, Costalot and Spendit. (You may want up to four shops if you feel that there will be traffic flow problems.) Place the boxes, bottles and tubes in the shop, and tell the children that these represent the items for sale. Price up the items in the second shop, limiting the cost of each to whatever number additions you wish the children to learn.

What to do
Teach the children about the type of additions that you are focusing on, for example: number bonds (24 + 36), adding numbers with 9 or 8 as the last digit (19 + 26) or to bridge 'over' into a three-digit figure (60 + 57).

Instruct the children to write a price on a sticky label and to put it on an item in the first shop, Costalot. The remaining items can have random numbers on them or can be differentiated by difficulty. Tell the children that they can now go shopping, picking up two items and taking them to their desk. There they write down and work out the cost of their shopping. Take it in turns to be shopkeepers.

Once they have done this, they can return their items to the shop and select two more. When you feel that the children are confident with what they are doing, ask them to mark a partner's work. Can they correct any errors and help their partner to see where they could improve?

Special support
A child with ASD will probably need help from a learning support assistant in dealing with the social interactions of shops. Use this *key worker* to *teach communication skills*, *teach turn taking* and to encourage *self-monitoring*.

Extension
Introduce some written problems – either create your own, using examples from your shops, Costalot and Spendit, or use photocopiable page 70. Allow the children to work them out. They can then write some of their own for their partners to solve.

Dramatic mathematics

Children with ASD may need a lot of support with understanding the abstract language of numberwork and algebra. This word-sorting game reinforces that understanding.

AGE RANGE
Seven to nine.

GROUP SIZE
Whole group, then pairs.

LEARNING OBJECTIVE FOR ALL THE CHILDREN
● To learn how to recognise which of the four rules to use when faced with a written problem.

INDIVIDUAL LEARNING TARGET
● To be able to match add/sum, subtract/take away, multiply/ times, divide/share and work practical examples.

What you need
Pelmanism cards (see below), two sets per pair; photocopiable page 70, one copy per pair; drama props (for example: shawls, hats, pretend or real food items); colouring pencils.

Preparation
The children should have covered all four mathematics rules before this lesson. Prepare some pairs of Pelmanism cards with words linked to the four operations, for example: 'take away' and 'subtract'; 'divide' and 'share'; 'total' and 'sum'. Create a drama space at the front of the classroom.

What to do
This activity is useful to sort out confusion over which rules to apply, and uses mathematics in an everyday context. With the children go through the key vocabulary needed to identify which of the four rules they should use, and point out that there are some words that can be used for any of the four rules, for example, 'total'.

Let the children play a game of 'Pelmanism' or 'Pairs', in which a set of cards is scattered face down on a table. The first player picks up two of the cards. If they form a matching pair (for example, 'add' and 'plus'), then they keep them and have another turn. If they do not, then they replace them in exactly the same place and the second player has a turn. This continues until all of the pairs have been found. (The same game can be used to pair opposites.)

Introduce the 'Solve it!' problem sheet on page 70. Tell the children that these are all practical problems, but are presented in written form. In pairs, the children should underline in one colour the numbers that are involved. Point out that they may be hidden, for example, 'week'. Then, the children should take a second colour and underline the word or phrase that tells them which rule to use. Go through the first one with them, picking out the numbers they need and then searching for the word(s) that tell what to do with the numbers.

Special support
This activity is helpful for teaching *turn taking* and taking advantage of a *buddy system* when selecting partners. Teach and support abstract vocabulary and *keep it concrete* if you need to by using concrete counters.

Extension
Help the children make up their own problems to perform.

Amrit needed two more stickers to complete his book. They cost _____ each. What was the total cost of the stickers?

	+		=	

AGE RANGE
Nine to eleven.

GROUP SIZE
Whole group, then pairs.

LEARNING OBJECTIVE FOR ALL THE CHILDREN
● To understand how to use and interpret symbols in mathematical problems.

INDIVIDUAL LEARNING TARGET
● To calculate a simple algorithm, for example: 3 y = 9.

Transforming robots

Children who find it hard to grasp abstract concepts are sometimes particularly challenged by algebra in the early stages. Here is an idea for making the task personally meaningful for the child with ASD.

What you need
Toy robot, preferably one that can transform; Post-it Notes; individual whiteboards and pens.

Preparation
The children should have covered all four rules before this lesson.

What to do
Start with the warm-up activity 'Guess my numbers'. Tell the children that you have a number, for example 20. Ask the children different ways of making 20, such as 4 x 5, 14 + 6, 100 ÷ 5, 32 – 12. Allow the children to ask the class ways of making other numbers. Highlight the main teaching point: that the four rules can be used to find different numbers.

Show the children a number sentence, such as: 3 + ? = 11. If they want to find the missing number, what do they have to do? Give them a variety of examples that use all four rules and teach the children how to work these out. Particularly reinforce the point that both sides of an equation are equal. Tell them that sometimes a symbol is put instead of a box.

Introduce Tommy Transformer (a robot). Ask four children to come up in front of the class with individual whiteboards. Each whiteboard offers one part of a number sentence, such as the one above. The unknown number for the moment is stuck on Tommy's back. Put different algebraic number sentences on the boards, always hiding Tommy's number behind him. Let the children work out what number he is hiding before revealing the number.

When you are happy that the children have grasped the idea, give out the Post-it Notes for the children to draw their own symbols. Then let them make up number sentences for a partner, putting their Post-it symbol over one of the numbers. Can their partners work it out?

Special support
Spend quite a while with the child with ASD setting the problems for the partner to solve, before switching roles. That way, you are making use of *good role models* and *being patient* as they grasp the rules of the game.

Extension
Teach the children to continue making up their own problems for others to work out.

Grab a grobble

Number skills can be a real strength for the child with ASD. This activity allows you to celebrate that fact!

AGE RANGE
Seven to nine.

GROUP SIZE
Whole group, then pairs.

LEARNING OBJECTIVE FOR ALL THE CHILDREN
● To investigate prime numbers and factors.

INDIVIDUAL LEARNING TARGET
● To calculate in front of a large group.

What you need
A bag of Unifix cubes (or similar) per pair; recording sheet, one per pair.

Preparation
Make up a recording sheet (see diagram, below), allowing for at least ten turns.

What to do
This activity engages children in a range of multiplication and division skills that helps them to find and understand factors, multiples and prime numbers. You may wish to reveal this objective later in the lesson.

Tell the children that they are to play a game in pairs called 'Grab a grobble'. Explain that one 'grobble' is a Unifix cube (or whatever you have chosen). Each child dips into the bag with one hand and grabs a number of grobbles (for example, 15). Using a recording chart they see which of the timestables go into (or are a factor of) 15. Award a point for each factor. Warn them that there will be some 'good' numbers that will score lots of points and some 'lazy' numbers that will not score them any points! (These are the prime numbers.) Put the grobbles back after each turn. After five turns, allow the children to use two hands to generate larger numbers.

Add up the total number of points after ten turns. Tell the children to identify which numbers were 'good' and which were 'lazy'. Put these up on the board in any order in two separate lists. What can the children say about these numbers? Can they find any pattern with the numbers that gave four points? Is there a 'rule' for the 'lazy' numbers?

Number of grobbles	x 2?	x 3?	x 4?	x 5?	x 6?	x 7?	x 8?	x 9?	x 10?	Points
Turn 1 =15		Yes 1		Yes 1						2
Turn 2										
Turn 3										

Finally, ensure that the children understand that they have found prime numbers and numbers that have plenty of factors.

Special support
Use a *key worker* to work with the child with ASD at first to help them grasp the procedure. Then introduce a partner and use this as an opportunity to *encourage communication* and *teach turn taking*.

Extension
Using the information from this investigation, children can go on to find the remaining prime numbers up to 100.

Dramatic mathematics

Don bought a comic from the newsagent's. It cost £1.75. Next he went to the corner shop to buy a chocolate bar that cost 99p. How much was his shopping altogether?

Yasmin loves cakes. She went to the baker's and bought a cream bun for 57p and a doughnut for 42p. She added the prices to find out how much the cakes were altogether.

Amrit needed two more stickers to complete his book. They cost 60p each. What was the total cost of the stickers?

Ellie bought two tickets for the show, one for her and one for her grandma. Looking at the poster, she saw children paid £10 and adults paid £20. What was the total cost of the tickets?

Hyun needed food for his dog and cat. The pet shop sells all types of food.
Dog food – £1.85
Cat food – £1.30
Fish food – £1.49
What was the sum of Hyun's shopping?

Leroy wanted to buy presents for his mum and dad. He found a comb priced 99p and a pack of cards at £1.75. He had £2.85. Did he have enough money?

Jim worked for one week at a rate of £25 a day. How much did he earn?

Peter was given £10 for his birthday. He spent £7.50 at the shops. How much money did he have left?

After the film, there were 15 sweets left in the bag. The three friends wanted to share them out equally. How many should each friend have?

Ella counted 13 children in the swimming pool. Then she saw 6 children get out. How many were left swimming?

Can you write out a problem for a friend to work out?

SPECIAL NEEDS in the primary years: Autistic Spectrum Difficulties

INFORMATION AND COMMUNICATION TECHNOLOGY

ICT is a strand of the National Curriculum in which many children with ASD can excel. Again, your task becomes one of helping these children use systems, not just for their own sake (excellent and stress-relieving though that may be) but as practical applications to real-life enquiries and problems. The *use of ICT* is predictable and logical and follows set routines, all of which are likely to appeal to children with ASD. However, the children can become very absorbed when using ICT tools, so the activities in this section help you to plan lessons where ICT is used appropriately and usefully.

Sometimes children with ASD become easily distracted in class and find it hard to concentrate if a computer screen is visible – look for ways of *removing distractions* and screening computers off in work areas. When using the computer for a set task, the child might 'go off on a tangent' and be completely oblivious to the fact that you set them a very different task to do. You will need to practise *being patient* and setting *clear expectations*, returning from time to time and *giving feedback* on how they are meeting the aims of the task. Try to select software that minimises distractions, and help the child to maintain focus by providing a visually presented set of steps to follow. Structured worksheets or Word pages can be given for the child to complete following their task.

Some children with ASD have been able to contribute very effectively to class topic work through searching the web. However, the pupil might have difficulty in selecting the various options when using the web – provide key words and criteria for the child to apply. Try to pre-programme their thinking and attention towards the task in hand and take trouble to show *why* the task is relevant.

Computers are an effective means of learning and recording for children with ASD since they are visual, predictable, make no social demands and are intrinsically rewarding. Since communication is a central difficulty for pupils with ASD, it can be very helpful for them if they learn to feel comfortable communicating by email, e-discussion group or text. Again, try to make this meaningful, perhaps by pairing up pupils to communicate messages and information to each other. Partners can be encouraged to share activities at the computer as a way of *teaching turn taking*, and you can use egg-timers or *visual timetables* to provide *warnings* of when the ICT task will end. ICT can also be a useful alternative if there are pencil control difficulties, since keyboards and a mouse are generally easier to manipulate.

Colour it happy

Children with ASD might be really attracted to computers and learn to excel when using them. However, they might need help to use ICT creatively and flexibly.

AGE RANGE
Five to seven.

GROUP SIZE
Small group.

LEARNING OBJECTIVE FOR ALL THE CHILDREN
● To try things out on the computer and explore what happens.

INDIVIDUAL LEARNING TARGET
● To create a colourful design using the computer.

What you need
Computers; computer graphics program, such as RM Colour Magic; colour printer; A4 paper.

Preparation
Familiarise the children with the basic features of a computer graphics program and make sure the children can select and draw an outline shape, using the mouse and dragging; fill a shape; change the fill colour.

What to do
Explain that you are going to make an abstract picture. Children with ASD are often unsure of anything abstract, so you may need to call it a pattern or an experiment. Talk a little bit about the meaning of 'edges' and 'boundaries'. Illustrate on the board how a new shape can be created by overlapping two other shapes.

Using the graphics program, ask the children to draw ten circles (one for each finger and thumb), so that they overlap and cover the whole drawing area. Many children with ASD find choice difficult so, by prescribing the shape and number, you have given them the close guidelines they need to get started.

Ask the children to fill in all the shapes they have created in different colours, so that no shape is touched by another shape of the same colour. Children with ASD enjoy repetition and are usually happy to repeat the same shape, but other children can be offered more variety if you wish.

All children will respond to the challenge of being creative within the limitations you set. Meanwhile, you can cover some valuable shape vocabulary without them noticing.

Special support
Keep it concrete by giving precise instructions and setting *clear expectations*. If appropriate, give the child *special responsibility* to teach a basic ICT skill to a partner. This can also give you the chance to *teach turn taking*.

Extension
This is a useful activity as it can be differentiated and extended easily by varying the shapes (for example: three triangles, two circles, four squares and a star); selecting different colours (for example: only red, blue and green); or suggesting different sizes (for example: three big, three small, three medium and one tiny).

AGE RANGE
Five to seven.

GROUP SIZE
Small group.

LEARNING OBJECTIVE FOR ALL THE CHILDREN
● To select from, and add to, information they have retrieved for particular purposes.

INDIVIDUAL LEARNING TARGET
● To use ICT to complete a simple set task.

Make a card

Children with ASD might become easily distracted by their own agenda when using ICT. This motivating activity keeps them focused on the task in hand.

What you need
Computers; Wordart or similar program; Clipart files; colour printer; good quality A4 paper or thin card; A6 envelopes; a greetings card with vertical and horizontal folds for demonstration.

Preparation
Ensure that the children know how to: import a picture, position and resize it; turn text; change page view; fold a piece of paper into four. Set the computers to 'whole page' within the page view before the children begin the activity. This will help them to place the graphics correctly on their greetings cards.

What to do
Talk about birthdays and celebrations and other times you might want to send a card. Ask who the children would like to send a card to and why. Hold up a greetings card and ask what they notice about it. Talk about the outside, inside, back, front, right, left, picture, greeting, and so on. You might find it necessary to guide the child with ASD into understanding the connection between opposites by saying, for example: 'If John can see the front, what can Daisy see?' Avoid using 'I' and 'you' as some ASD children get confused, as pronouns do not always refer to the same person.

Explain that to get the card 'right', everything has to be in the correct place. Unfold the greetings card to show how it is made from one sheet of paper. Prompt the children until they notice that part of it is upside down. Ask how they might be able to do that on the computer.

Ask the children to import a picture and size it in the bottom right-hand corner of the screen. Then let them write their text in Word Art and position it upside down in the top-left quadrant. It might be helpful to have a diagram for them to follow.

Once the children have completed their design, let them print out their page and fold it correctly into a card. Children are often fascinated to see their finished greeting card, which could then be taken home.

Special support
Set *clear expectations* and *avoid ambiguity* by giving the child a clearly defined end product to achieve. Consider using *taped texts* to serve as instructions for certain children with ASD.

Extension
Teach the children to prepare an address label on an A6 envelope to complete the activity.

AGE RANGE
Seven to nine.

GROUP SIZE
Small group.

LEARNING OBJECTIVE FOR ALL THE CHILDREN
● To learn how to navigate to a particular website and to carry out a speaking and listening group survival exercise once there.

INDIVIDUAL LEARNING TARGET
● To navigate the web to find a simple piece of information.

Internet survivor

Children with ASD can use the internet for simple research if they are helped to focus their attentions. Here is an activity to teach them the basics.

What you need
Computers with internet access.

Preparation
Ensure that the computers can access the Eden Project activity and familiarise yourself with the layout. This activity could be set up as a speaking and listening activity and linked to work in science (for example, 'Habitats'), or as an ICT internet skills lesson.

Familiarise yourself with the selected website – particularly if you are going to guide the children through a search for it. The Eden Project's 'Don't forget your leech socks' activity can be accessed at **www.learn.co.uk/edenproject/workshops/leech** (Check periodically that the activity can be found in the same location.)

What to do
Put the children into groups of three to six, with one computer per group. Inform the children that they are scientists about to go on an expedition into a rainforest. They will need to search the internet to find out what equipment they must take. Teach the children how to open the internet and how to use a search engine. Give them some particular sites to find and visit.

Once you are sure they are confident in using the computer, ask them to find a website relating to the Eden Project, which gives details about their expedition. Depending on their level of expertise, either direct them to *Learn → Eden Project → Can't go → Don't Forget Your Leech Socks → Click here to go to the Rainforest → Equipment Store*, or just give them a clue, such as 'Leeches'.

When they have found the equipment store, tell the children that they are going to make decisions about which equipment to take into the rainforest. Make sure that the children have different roles within their group (for example: chairperson, computer operator, observer, team member), so that they are all involved with the work.

Having decided on their equipment, the children can compare their selections with those of the experts. This might well produce even more discussion!

Special support
Prepare for this activity by using a *key worker* to talk through the idea of rainforests and expeditions with the child with ASD.

Extension
The children can go on to research the remainder of the website, collecting details about rainforests (for example, food chains, habitats, plants, and so on).

Email a leg!

Children with ASD might find that communicating with ICT is easier for them than face to face. Their arousal stays lower and the pace can be slowed down to suit them.

AGE RANGE
Seven to nine.

GROUP SIZE
Small group in pairs.

LEARNING OBJECTIVE FOR ALL THE CHILDREN
● To learn how to use attachments within emails to make up a 'Picasso'-style body shape.

INDIVIDUAL LEARNING TARGET
● To communicate with one other pupil using email or e-discussion group.

What you need
Access to a computer suite with emails and Clipart software set up for children; copies of Picasso pictures.

Preparation
Ensure the computer applications have Clip-art packages with different body parts that the children can copy. Pictures of Picasso paintings can be obtained from art books and journals, or on the internet through websites such as 'Google images'.

What to do
Put the children into pairs. Look at some of the Picasso paintings and discuss the way that he creates unusual pictures through placing parts of the body in different ways. Show the children how to send an email, send an attachment and copy and paste Clipart.

Tell the children that they are now going to send emails to each other, requesting different Clipart parts for their body pictures (for example: head, hair, right leg). You might want them to ask in order around the room so that everyone gets an equal number of requests. The children should keep on emailing requests until they have all the body parts they need.

On receiving a request, the children working in pairs find the body part they wish to send and copy it on to a new file using a text box. They should then name the file for the recipient and send it.

When the children have received all their body parts, they then copy and paste them all into one document. If the program has the facility to combine images they can create their 'Picasso' on screen. If not, they should print off all the images they now have. They can then cut them out and arrange them to create a colourful, imaginative display. Any that are completed on a computer could be sent to the teacher or parents via email for comments.

Special support
Use this activity to *teach communication skills* and *encourage communication*. Encourage the child to wait patiently for replies, as well as sending off requests.

Extension
Children can create stories based around a 'Consequences' game with sentences emailed to each other.

AGE RANGE
Nine to eleven.

GROUP SIZE
Whole group in groups, then pairs.

LEARNING OBJECTIVE FOR ALL THE CHILDREN
● To work within a speaking and listening group to conduct topic research on the internet.

INDIVIDUAL LEARNING TARGET
● To use ICT to contribute information towards a common goal.

Jigsaw research

It might be possible to involve the child with ASD fully in group research, using ICT to gather information on a set project or theme. Here is an idea for setting up a pupil 'research team'.

What you need
Internet computer access for whole class.

Preparation
Ensure that the computers can access particular sites you wish to research. Split the class up into jigsaw groups (see *National Literacy Strategy Speaking, Listening, Learning* 2003 for more information) of up to six pupils.

What to do
This activity is designed to teach both research and group skills and can be conducted over several lessons. It will help children with ASD, who often have good ICT ability, to contribute effectively to a group project.

Tell the class that they will use the internet to research a variety of topics, for example: Romans, Victorians, Plants or Animals.

Decide on four or five areas that the class will need to research within the topic. For example, for the topic of 'Romans', you could select Roman roads, Roman army, Roman games, Roman clothing and Roman inventions. Organise the children into 'home groups' and tell them that their job is to complete a report based on these five areas. To make it easier, they are going to appoint experts from their group to research one section.

Having decided an expert in each area, they then form 'expert groups' with children from other groups. They will need to work on computers in pairs but can swap websites and information within their expert group.

When the expert groups have managed to find and note all of their required information, they then come back to their home group and feed back. This should help to foster confidence within the group as each group member is an 'expert' in one area. The home group can then work on their report both together and individually to produce a final report.

Special support
Give the child with ASD the *special responsibility* of researching an area of interest to them and *teach communication skills* as they learn to share their information with others.

Extension
Encourage the children to extend their research to other areas of interest to them. Suggest that this approach is used for other class projects in the future.

The wind hissed!

It might be possible to encourage the child with ASD to write more creatively and productively using word-processing. Here is an activity to encourage prose writing.

AGE RANGE
Nine to eleven.

GROUP SIZE
Any.

LEARNING OBJECTIVE FOR ALL THE CHILDREN
● To use a mind map to assist in the drafting and ordering of a poem based around the use of personification.

INDIVIDUAL LEARNING TARGET
● To produce a passage of creative writing using word-processing.

What you need
Copies of the poem 'The wind hissed' (see photocopiable page 78); access to computers, one per pair; mind mapping software, such as MindManager® Pro; Clipart or Wordart package.

Preparation
Ensure that the computers have a suitable Clipart or Wordart package, as well as suitable mind mapping software installed.

What to do
Read as a class the poem 'The wind hissed'. Point out to the children the use of personification, which is the act of ascribing human characteristics to an idea or object, for example, the wind. Tell the children that they are now going to produce their own poem using 'The wind hissed' as a model. They will use mind maps to help them plan their poem and then word process a final version.

First, ask the children to decide on which objects they wish to feature in their poems (for example, a stone or a tree). Brainstorm a class list – these will form the main branches of the mind map and eventually the different lines of the poem.

Then, let the children decide on the human attributes they will ascribe to the object – these will form the sub-branches. At the moment, as it is a draft, they might put in a couple of words and decide later which one is best. They will need to go through each of these steps for all of the branches they create and then decide which order the lines should be put in (see the diagram below for an example).

Using copy and paste from their mind maps, the children can then produce a final version of the poem. The use of different fonts or text effects for different words may amplify the personification, and the use of Clipart might also enhance the appearance of the poem.

Special support
Use structure to break the task down and *keep it concrete* so that the child with ASD understands what to do at each step. The use of figurative language helps children with ASD to think more flexibly.

Extension
Ask the children to create a piece of narrative description that contains personification.

```
                    subtopic

  galloping              writhing
  gobbling               chomping

  waves      cliffs           sea
        ┌─────────────────────┐
        │ Personification Poem │
        │    - Coastline       │
        └─────────────────────┘
  sand                    rocks
    subtopic          shivered
    subtopic          crept
                      rumbled
                      leapt
```

The wind hissed

Scared was I as I crept through the streets,
The wind hissed,
Rain muttered,
Shop doors scowled,
On, on I stuttered.

Scared was I as I crept through the streets,
The windows glared,
Skyscrapers leered,
Drains gaped,
Everything I feared.

Scared was I as I crept through the streets,
The alleys howled,
Pavements swallowed,
Gutters spat,
Was I being followed?

Scared was I as I crept through the streets,
The signs stared,
Streetlamps stood,
Home stretched too far away,
Make it? Do you think I could...?

Andy Ogden

MUSIC

There is an approach called *musical interaction* therapy that was developed at Sutherland House School for children with ASD in Nottingham. It uses music to develop communication skills, recognising that communication follows an intricate web of giving and receiving in which people negotiate what they need to say, how to say it, and how to listen. Music can be used to develop this two-way process and is an excellent way of delivering the curriculum across many strands. In this section, there are ideas to start you off both in teaching music (where children with ASD can excel) and also using musical methods to teach other learning skills across the whole curriculum.

The teaching approaches used in *musical interaction* involve using music and song for *engaging attention*, such as in singing greeting songs and in personalised action songs at KS1 (for example, 'We have a friend and his name is *Wesley*, Hello *Wesley*, how are you?' and 'Will is *jumping*, Will is *jumping*, so is Ben, so is Ben…'). You can leave dramatic pauses in a song before an important key word in order to encourage a child with ASD to complete the word or phrase (for example, using just the start of a word, or a look, or a sign). Key words can be emphasised and taught with an action ('Then there were FORTY… ten, twenty, thirty, FORTY', holding up number cards), so that children with ASD can link an abstract concept with concrete action.

At KS2, music can provide a motivation and attention-holder that helps children with ASD stay relaxed and more able to interact socially, even in a large group. Music can focus attention and prevent the child becoming over-aroused so that you can make social demands on them more easily. Timestables can be sung and chanted to support everyone's learning. Theme-related background music can be used to support practical work during a project. Even in potentially threatening situations, such as assembly, the participation in a musical activity or band can provide the child who has ASD with a 'job to do' in what otherwise might be a very alarming situation.

Some children with ASD have exceptional abilities in areas not affected by communication and social behaviour. Music is one of these, and you might be able to provide opportunities for the child to succeed publicly in a very appropriate way. This can provide them with something to share with other like-minded pupils and is helpful for building confidence, self-esteem, teamwork and friendship skills.

AGE RANGE
Five to seven.

GROUP SIZE
Whole group.

LEARNING OBJECTIVE FOR ALL THE CHILDREN
● To play tuned and untuned instruments and rehearse and perform with others.

INDIVIDUAL LEARNING TARGET
● To tolerate and begin to join in a large-group activity.

Play the tambourine

Musical *circle time* is an excellent way to encourage social skills in children with ASD. Keep the routine safe and predictable.

What you need
Large box with enough tambourines or other appropriate instruments for one between three children.

Preparation
Collect the instruments and put them in the box.

What to do
When everybody is seated in a circle, chant or sing the following, with the children repeating each line back to you:
Music time
What shall we play?
We will play the tambourine.

Present the tambourine. Explain that an important part of playing music is being able to hold a musical instrument without making a sound. Tell the children to pass the tambourine round noiselessly. This quiet period allows the child with ASD to adjust visually and emotionally to what is going on. Passing to your right helps to reinforce the direction necessary for reading.

Next, demonstrate some of the sounds the tambourine can make. Talk to the children about the importance of the right sound at the right time, and that they can practise with imaginary tambourines. Say: 'You have all held the tambourine now. We are going to shake it and pass it on. What are we going to do?' Encourage the children to mime the actions. Model this with the real tambourine. This is important for the child with ASD as it allows for anticipation.

Give every third child a tambourine. Say: 'Shake the tambourine and pass it on.' Every child should have two turns miming and one hands-on experience. Repeat with: 'Tap the tambourine and pass it on' and 'Scrape the tambourine and pass it on.'

Finish by singing together: 'We can play on the tambourine and this is the way we do it' (shake, tap or scrape and pass it on). This time, when the tambourine reaches you, put it back in the box.

Special support
Miming is a difficult skill for the child with ASD to learn, since it involves flexible and imaginative thought. *Keep it concrete* at first by making sure the child always has an instrument. Then use imitation or hand-over-hand prompting to teach the right movements.

Extension
Repeat this activity with other instruments and talk about the different ways in which you can make sounds.

AGE RANGE
Five to seven.

GROUP SIZE
Whole group.

LEARNING OBJECTIVE FOR ALL THE CHILDREN
● To create musical patterns.

INDIVIDUAL LEARNING TARGET
● To listen to sounds and make responses with a partner.

Echoes

Music is a useful way of encouraging listening and responding so that the child with ASD learns the two-way process of conversation and communication. Here is an activity to encourage that.

What you need
Instruments (for example: shakers, triangles, drums, blocks, bells and tambourines), at least two of each sort.

Preparation
Create a screen (such as a table on its side) behind which a child can sit with a selection of hidden instruments. Select two identical sets of instruments; place one set behind the screen and one in front.

What to do
Sit the children in a semicircle and start an echo saying, 'Hello' and then repeating it more slowly – 'Hel-lo' Vary the pitch and volume of each syllable and ask the children to mimic. Repeat with 'Welcome', tapping your thighs in time with the syllables.

Now tell the children that you are going to change the game. Continue the tapping and add another short phrase, such as: 'How are you today?' If they mimic the phrase, stop them and joke: 'What do you usually say when someone asks how you are?' Talk about how, when somebody says something and another person replies, sometimes a phrase is repeated and sometimes it is not. If it is a *question*, then it needs a *reply*.

Invite a child to sit behind the screen, so that the other children cannot see what instrument is chosen. Tell the child to choose an instrument and make a four-beat sound with it. Ask a child from the semicircle to choose the same type of instrument from those in front of the screen and reply. Another pair can continue the activity.

There are plenty of variations to this activity, for example the child behind the screen could continue playing until they hear the same instrument 'replying'; the child then changes instruments and plays until the new instrument replies.

Special support
Engage attention by using the child's name before they are required to listen. If the child finds it difficult to make a choice when listening, *keep it concrete* by playing two instruments until the child chooses the correct one. This activity makes good use of *musical interactions*.

Extension
The instructions to the lead player can be varied, using vocabulary such as: loud, soft, quick, slow, clattery and so on. Alternatively, the children in the semicircle can all have instruments, but only one child plays their particular instrument when they hear it being played from behind the screen.

AGE RANGE
Seven to nine.

GROUP SIZE
Whole group.

LEARNING OBJECTIVE FOR ALL THE CHILDREN
● To write lyrics to help learn the 3- and 4-times tables.

INDIVIDUAL LEARNING TARGET
● To chant a musical timestable.

Musical multiplying

Music can be enjoyed in its own right and also used as a vehicle for teaching other curricular skills. Here is a musical timestable activity.

What you need
Copy of the nursery rhyme *One, Two Buckle My Shoe*; rhyming dictionaries, for example: *The Penguin Rhyming Dictionary* by Rosalind Fergusson (Penguin).

Preparation
Write or display the rhyme *One Two Buckle My Shoe* on the board. Prepare some initial ideas for the whole-class rhyme.

What to do
Read together the nursery rhyme *One, Two Buckle My Shoe*. Read it through again, clapping on the numbers. Ask the class why they think young children are taught this rhyme. Why does the rhyme help children to learn? Ask if the children know the actions for each part and why they think actions are used with young children.

Tell the children that they are going to use the same pattern to create their own timestable songs. Take them through the structure of the rhyme, for example: two numbers followed by a three- or four-syllable line. Ask the children to tell you which two words in each verse rhyme.

Together, write out the 3-times table together in pairs of numbers on the board. Make sure you leave a line under each pair to fit the rhyme in. Start with 'Three, six' and then ask for words that rhyme. (Use the rhyming dictionaries, if necessary.) Ask the children to consider how many syllables fit best. Can the children decide upon a rhyme for which they can also include an action?

As a class, complete the rest of the timestable up to 30 and practise it together. Put the children in pairs and give them time to learn and practise the rhyme. Then, with close adult support, let them take turns to perform it together.

Special support
If this activity is too wordy, simply recite a timestable to music (for example, the 2-times table to the tune of *Twinkle Twinkle Little Star*) and tape it for the child to listen and learn. *Taped texts*, especially set to music, are a useful memory aid.

Extension
The children could choose or invent a tune to sing their rhyme to. They could also make up their own rhyme for the 4-times table to use in the next mathematics lesson.

AGE RANGE
Seven to nine.

GROUP SIZE
Whole group.

LEARNING OBJECTIVE FOR ALL THE CHILDREN
● To be able to identify and express feelings within music.

INDIVIDUAL LEARNING TARGET
● To use instruments to express anger, happiness and sorrow.

Musical moods

It can be very hard for a child with ASD to understand feelings in themselves and others. This activity links music with feelings and provides opportunities for sharing feelings with others.

What you need
CD player or tape recorder; selection of music that exemplifies different moods for example: (*calm*) *Pavane* by Fauré (from, for example, *Choral Works*, EMI), (*excitement*) *Let Me Entertain You* by Robbie Williams (Chrysalis), (*anger*) 'Mars, 'the Bringer of War' from *The Planets* by Holst (for example, EMI), (*peaceful*) *Albatross* by Fleetwood Mac (Sony); selection of musical instruments, percussion and tuned; emotions cards, one per child (see 'Making faces on page 48).

Preparation
Allow the children to practise using some of the instruments before the lesson. Prepare and copy a 'Musical moods listening sheet' – one sheet per child (see diagram, below).

What to do
Play the children several of the pieces of music you have selected. Ask them to register the feelings suggested to them by the music. Take two pieces that are very different. Play them again, one at a time. Ask the children, while you are doing this, to complete the listening sheets – drawing in the box and writing words on the branches around the picture about what they feel is suggested by the music.

Give out the emotions cards, one to each child. Tell them not to show their card to anyone.

Invite the children to look at the range of instruments that are in the room and decide which one would match the word that they have been given. Let the children practise using the instruments for a short time and then ask individuals to come to the front and play their chosen instrument to convey the emotion on their card. See if the other children can guess which emotion is being played.

Special support
Help the child with ASD to think more flexibly by leading them through any intermediate steps. For example, read an emotions card together. Name the emotion (for example, anger). Ask the child to demonstrate how that feels (such as tensing up fingers and arms). Now tell them to stay tense and play the instrument.

Extension
Encourage some of the children to use the tuned instruments to create a longer piece to play to the class to express an emotion.

Musical moods listening sheet

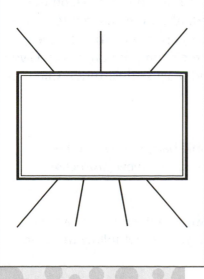

AGE RANGE
Nine to eleven.

GROUP SIZE
Whole group, in pairs.

LEARNING OBJECTIVE FOR ALL THE CHILDREN
● To compose a tuned piece of music to known words.

INDIVIDUAL BEHAVIOUR TARGET
● To compose a short passage of music.

Tuneful traffic

Music can be used to help children with ASD think more flexibly and creatively. This activity encourages creativity, yet has a structured framework for supporting a child with ASD.

What you need
Half-class set of xylophones or chime bars; musical notation sheets, one per pair (see photocopiable page 86).

Preparation
Write the words of the Green Cross Code on the board (see photocopiable page 86).

What to do
Tell your class that the Green Cross Code needs a catchy jingle to help children remember it. There are words already, but the children need to write a tune for it. This can be done over a series of lessons.

Prepare the children to work in four-beat bars by using clapping rhythms. Count in even time as you do so, 'One, two, three, four.' Now introduce two beats where there seems to be a pause. Explain that the note is still being played. Clap different patterns where the double beat might come on the second or third beat, for example: *single, single, double* or *single, double single* or *double double*. Get the children to clap back to you. Ask different children to clap a rhythm that the class reply to by copying.

Position a xylophone behind a desk where the children cannot see the notes you are playing. Play two notes and ask whether they are higher, lower or the same in pitch. Now play the clapping game again, except this time using your xylophone, with the children guessing which pattern you have played.

Introduce the children to the notation sheet. The children will only work in single beats (crotchets) and double beats (minims). They will only use a pentatonic scale of A, C, D, E and G. (These are used as they will always sound in tune.) Use the example on the sheet to show how this will be played. Allow the children to try out different tunes to the words on their xylophones. When satisfied, they should note down the tune on their composition sheets. Give the children time in pairs to learn and practise their tunes. Can they perform them to the class?

Special support
If you have xylophones with removable bars, remove all the unwanted bars for pupils who need you to *remove distractions*.

Extension
The children could add some percussion to their tune or write a second verse – what might happen if you do not follow the Green Cross Code!

Musical notation

Example		Beat		
	1	2	3	4
A	♩			
C		♩	♩	♩
D				
E				
G				

	1	2	3	4
A				
C				
D				
E				
G				
	Look	left	Look	right

	1	2	3	4
A				
C				
D				
E				
G				
	Look	left	a -	gain

	1	2	3	4
A				
C				
D				
E				
G				
	Cross	o -	ver	now

AGE RANGE
Nine to eleven.

GROUP SIZE
Whole-class assembly; groups of four to six on compositional tasks.

LEARNING OBJECTIVE FOR ALL THE CHILDREN
● To compose music and perform a class assembly based around *The Snow Dragon*.

INDIVIDUAL LEARNING TARGET
● To work as a full member of a team.

Dragon tales

Musical ensemble work provides an excellent opportunity for developing teamwork and mutual cooperation for the child with ASD.

What you need
Half-class set of xylophones or chime bars; musical notation sheets – one per group (see photocopiable page 86 and Tuneful traffic lesson on page 84); lots of percussion instruments; copies of *The Snow Dragon* by Vivian French, illustrated by Chris Fisher (Corgi).

Preparation
This activity is a sequence over couple of weeks. Set up separate areas of the room, and group your class for different compositional activities. Prepare a summary of the story. This activity could be adapted for a variety of texts – *The Snow Dragon* is used as a model.

What to do
Read *The Snow Dragon* to the children. Make sure they know the story well. Tell them they are going to compose music to go with this story. They will need to work as groups in the following areas:
Snow Dragons: a refrain or chorus to cue to the audience that the Snow Dragon is in this scene. They will need to use the xylophones, write music using the notation sheets and compose their own lyrics.
Fire Dragons: a refrain or chorus as for the Snow Dragons.
Percussion Group One: sounds for the 'First Happening', where the Fire Dragons drive out the Twolegs and Snow Dragons.
Percussion Group Two: sounds for when Little Tuft meets Book.
Percussion Group Three: sounds for the scene where Little Tuft visits the Snow Dragon.
Percussion Group Four: sounds for the scene where Little Tuft flies with the Snow Dragon.
Percussion Group Five: sounds for the battle scene between the Snow Dragons and Fire Dragons.
Additional Sounds Group: for particular sounds during any of the scenes, for example, a snicker for Book.
   Give the children time in groups to prepare, practise and learn their parts, including the voices. Once the work is complete, arrange for the children to play their composition in an assembly.

Special support
If necessary, use a *key worker* to support certain groups and use *interpretation* to *teach communication skills* and to *encourage communication* as the child with ASD begins to learn how to work as part of a team.

Extension
Early finishers might compose an introduction for the audience for when they arrive.

Musical notation

Example

Beat

Note	1	2	3	4
A	♩		♩	
C		♩		♩
D				
E				
G				

Note	1	2	3	4
A				
C				
D				
E				
G				

| | Look | left | Look | right |

Note	1	2	3	4
A				
C				
D				
E				
G				

| | Look | left | a - | gain |

Note	1	2	3	4
A				
C				
D				
E				
G				

| | Cross | o - | ver | now |

PHYSICAL EDUCATION

One of the greatest challenges when including children with ASD is helping them manage their anxiety and time during unstructured breaks and dinner hours. Children with ASD find it hard to cope when there is no predictability and routine, and they can quickly become stressed. At the same time, it would be counter-productive to exclude them from these situations since they can provide such good opportunities for developing communication, social behaviour and flexibility. That is why part of this section will focus on teaching and developing an ethos of playground games that can be used to introduce structure to breaktimes and outdoor play.

Children with ASD are more likely to benefit from learning these games in their routine PE lessons where they do not also have to cope with a large and busy playground. Playground games work best for children with ASD where an individual's role within the game is obvious. You will then need to support the development of these games in the actual situation of the playground in order for the child with ASD to generalise what has been learned and be prompted to join in. This can make an excellent whole-school project for all staff to become involved with and is well worth investing time in for the benefits of better behaviour and more inclusion.

Again, look for a balance between opportunities that playtime provides and the individual needs of the child with ASD. These children sometimes genuinely *need* to be on their own for at least part of playtime, as a respite from the social demands of the classroom. Make sure that the *safe base* is still available for them. It can also be helpful if the teacher on duty helps children with ASD observe how the other children are playing, talking them through what is happening. Sometimes it is possible to find a game that appeals to the observer and encourages them to join in with the teacher's support. Children with *Asperger's syndrome* are often desperate to join in but do not know how, and teaching them opening lines and introductions can be very helpful.

Children with ASD are sometimes rather clumsy in their movement and balance, and there are opportunities in PE for developing their skills, using solitary, though parallel, physical exercises as well as group and team games. Look for ways of helping these children develop skills when working individually (such as ball control or running) that they can then incorporate into a more social game.

Crossing the river

This simple game can be taught during PE and then supported during outdoor playtime, prompting any children with ASD to join in and enjoy the chase.

What you need
A large area, such as a hall or playground; tape or rope; PE bands, one per 'wildebeest'.

Preparation
Ask the children to wear their PE kit for this activity. Explain to the children that this is a *game*. Introduce and explain the vocabulary of 'wildebeest', 'migration' and 'alligator'. Mark out a 'river' centrally, using either tape or rope, approximately half the area available.

What to do
Tell the children that they are going to take on the parts of alligators or wildebeest. The wildebeest are going to cross the river and try to keep their tails. Show them the markings that represent the river. Pick some children to be the alligators. One alligator to about five or six wildebeest works quite well.

Line the wildebeest up along one edge of the river. Give the alligators the bands to give out to each wildebeest. (This encourages social skills and the concept of 'one each' among the children.) Each wildebeest tucks the top third of the band into the back of their PE shorts. Allow the alligators to slip into the water and patrol, eyeing up 'lunch'. (This gives time for the wildebeest to settle, tuck in their tails and think of tactics to avoid capture.)

Once they all have their tails tucked in, on a signal from you, they should run from one side of the river to the other. The alligators must stay in the river and collect as many tails as they can from the passing wildebeest.

When all the children are on the far bank, they check their tails. Those who have lost their tails are out of the game. Those who still have their tails may return across the river until there are the same number of wildebeest and alligators. The alligators then give the remaining wildebeest the bands they have captured and those children become the new alligators.

Special support
Introduce islands in the river – safety mats on which wildebeest can rest and not be captured. If necessary, lead a child with ASD by the hand until the rules of the game become a *familiar routine*.

Extension
Introduce the playground game of 'Tail tig'. Children play with a partner. One child wears the 'tail' and is chased by the partner. As soon as the tail is caught, they change roles.

Pass the ball

Children with ASD can be helped to join in simple ball games if you can teach them the skills involved and then provide a structured format for a game.

What you need
Four footballs, preferably of different colours; two hoops; sufficient space to play the game.

Preparation
The children should have practised controlling and passing a ball.

What to do
Divide the children into two equal teams. Divide each team again. Each team has half of its players standing in a row on each side of the 'playing area'. A hoop is placed centrally in line with each team.

The first child from each half-team dribbles the ball to the hoop. There will be four children with four balls moving. When each pair meet at the hoop, the ball is passed to the child coming from the opposite direction. That child continues to the other side where the ball is passed to the next child who is at the front of that group. The second child repeats the process. The game finishes when all the children are on the opposite side to the one from which they started. The first team to accomplish this wins the game.

Points to note: the children cross the complete space, but the balls only travel halfway and are brought back by the child from the opposite side of the play area. Coloured balls help to make this obvious. The only 'rule' is that the balls must come to rest in the hoop.

Special support
Use *traffic lights* to slow the game down if it becomes disorganised. *Catch the moment* to praise good *turn taking*.

Extension
Build the skills into a simple game of dribbling, goal-shooting and defending.

AGE RANGE
Five to seven.

GROUP SIZE
Whole group.

LEARNING OBJECTIVE FOR ALL THE CHILDREN
● To remember and repeat simple skills with increasing control and coordination.

INDIVIDUAL LEARNING TARGET
● To join in a simplified football game with a small team of other children.

direction of the ball

 player 1 (from the left)

 player 2 (from the right)

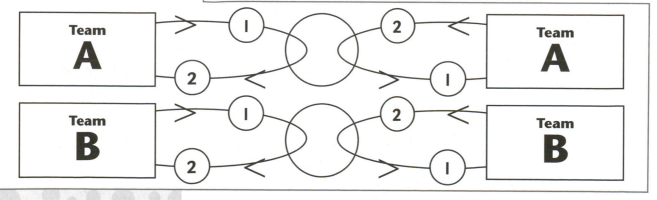

PHYSICAL EDUCATION · PHYSICAL EDUCATION

AGE RANGE
Seven to nine.

GROUP SIZE
Whole class in groups of three children.

LEARNING OBJECTIVE FOR ALL THE CHILDREN
● To throw a ball accurately underarm.

INDIVIDUAL LEARNING TARGET
● To throw a ball with approximate aim.

Beat the pit

Children with ASD are sometimes clumsy in their movements and do not seem to pick up physical skills by simply observing others. These activities will help them have greater success.

What you need
One hoop and six tennis balls per group; a rounders bat (optional); chalk.

Preparation
Lay out the hoops about three metres apart and place the six balls inside them. Mark a line with chalk from which the children will throw.

What to do
Teach and develop these activities over several sessions. Ask the children to work in groups of three.

Skills practice
The children take it in turns to throw the balls into the hoop. One child throws while another collects. The third stands by the hoop and counts how many are thrown into it.

Techniques
● The ball should be held in the fingertips to gain more control.
● The thumb should point forward with the fingers behind.
● The opposite foot to the throwing hand should be moved forward.
● The throwing arm should be relaxed and straight.
● The non-throwing arm should be out in front of the body, guiding the other hand towards the target. It pulls back as the throwing hand comes forward.

Beat the pit
In this game the children leave five balls in the hoop ('the pit'). They take the other ball to the throwing line. They then try to knock the five balls out of the hoop. They 'keep' any balls that they knock out. The end of the game comes either when all the balls have been knocked out or the children have each had ten throws.

Special support
At first, use larger balls and more of them, encouraging any child who is experiencing difficulties to stand closer to the hoop.

Extension
Encourage the children to stand further back. Invite one of the children to hold the hoop at their side at waist height. Challenge the other children to use a bat to hit the ball through the hoop. Alternatively, the children could play 'Beat the pit' with marbles in the playground.

Triathlon

It can be difficult for children with ASD to cope with the social demands of breaktime where there are no rules, a lot of noise and other children expect them to behave in ways they cannot understand. *Visual timetables* can really help.

AGE RANGE
Seven to nine.

GROUP SIZE
Whole class in groups of six to eight children.

LEARNING OBJECTIVE FOR ALL THE CHILDREN
● To understand instructions and to talk about 'tactics' to use in small games.

INDIVIDUAL LEARNING TARGET
● To use a visual timetable to structure playtime.

What you need
Hall or playground; chalk or masking tape; a soft ball (the size of a small football); two tennis balls.

Preparation
Prepare three separate areas with boundary markings and equipment for each game. For 'Four-square', you need to mark out a square 8m x 8m and split this into four smaller squares (see diagram on photocopiable page 94). Enlarge a set of instructions for each game and copy for each group (see photocopiable pages 94 and 95).

What to do
Split the class into at least three groups and organise each group into one of the separate areas. Let the children read the instructions for their game. Tell them they must discuss their game within their groups and work out how to play it, as they will have to teach it to other groups later. Each group then plays its game.

Move around the groups, ensuring that they are playing each game correctly. Give them time to explain the game to the other groups. Encourage the other children to ask questions if they do not understand any of the rules. Rotate the groups so that they are able to play all three games.

Special support
Now help a child with ASD plan a playground session by making a visual timetable with all three games on. Use it to suggest a list of 'things to do' within a group of friends or to allow the child to make choices. The equipment itself can serve as a *transfer* object from classroom to playground.

Extension
Encourage the children to teach other games that they play. They might also like to make up their own games. Sometimes children change the rules of a game as it goes along in order to improve it. Point out that they should make sure they explain clearly before they do.

AGE RANGE
Nine to eleven.

GROUP SIZE
Whole class in groups of six or seven children.

LEARNING OBJECTIVE FOR ALL THE CHILDREN
● To work as a team to overcome a variety of obstacles.

INDIVIDUAL LEARNING TARGET
● To listen to and share simple ideas within a small group.

Landlubbers

Children with ASD can be challenged by teamwork as they find it hard to take on board other people's points of view. This activity encourages teamwork and provides more ideas to help them develop imaginative playground games.

What you need
Hall or playground; three hoops (per group); two wooden planks and one bench (per group); video camera (optional).

Preparation
For the first activity, place the hoops at one end of the hall with the team of children. For the second activity, lay the benches halfway down the hall or playground lying across the group's path. Planks should be given to the children.

What to do
Put the children into groups of six or seven. If you have a video camera, film the children during these activities, as it is invaluable for the children to view playback of themselves working as a group.

First challenge
Explain to each group that they are landlubbers. They must work as a team to cross shark-infested waters using only three round 'stepping stones' (the hoops). If one team member so much as puts a toe in the 'water', they all have to jump back to the beginning. You may wish to make this competitive or leave it as an open, collaborative activity. Ask the other teams to watch each group of landlubbers to pick out good and poor examples of teamwork. Give the children time to discuss how they will set about their tasks before they begin. At the end, either replay the video or ask the observers and participants to evaluate the teamwork.

Second challenge
Tell the teams that they are also landlubbers. However, this time they must cross a piranha-infested river by using a movable raft (the two planks). A coral reef in the middle (the bench) must also be overcome, but can also be used to stand on. Go through the same procedure as for the first challenge. Again, ask if the teams learned anything that helped them work together better.

Special support
Start by pairing a child with ASD with a partner and providing extra supervision. *Catch the moment* when the pupil contributes or responds to an idea.

Extension
Children can invent their own challenge using different apparatus.

AGE RANGE
Nine to eleven.

GROUP SIZE
Whole class in groups of four children.

LEARNING OBJECTIVE FOR ALL THE CHILDREN
● To complete a gymnastic routine with other children a) one after the other b) at the same time.

INDIVIDUAL LEARNING TARGET
● To take part in a PE partner game for at least five minutes.

Cannon and synchronisation

Because of their difficulties in communication, turn-taking partner games can be used very helpfully for children with ASD. Here is an activity that can also be played in the playground.

What you need
Variety of simple gym equipment, for example: mats and low benches for all groups (it is not necessary for each group to have the same equipment); video player and video showing gymnasts or dancers performing; video camera (optional).

Preparation
Prepare a plan of the PE equipment. The children could design their own layout of the equipment to suit their routine. Show a video of gymnasts or dancers working in cannon and in synchronisation. The children should have reached a stage at which they have a variety of gymnastic skills available to them. Put the children into groups of four.

What to do
Explain the terms 'cannon' (one after the other, usually a beat later) and 'synchronisation' (at the same time). Show examples of both types of routine to the children. Tell them, that as a group, they will be designing their own simple gymnastic routines, beginning with cannon.

Warm up the groups by doing a 'Follow-my-leader', where the others copy the movements of the person in front (for example: walking, raising the left hand in the air and stopping to balance on one foot).

Introduce the apparatus the groups will use. Ask the children to discuss where they will place each item and then give them enough time to devise their routine and memorise it, making sure that it involves cannon.

The children can perform their routine to another group and gain constructive feedback from them. The class could then perform these routines to another class or in an assembly or as a special evening for parents and carers.

Special support
As a *motivator*, start by asking the child with ASD to perform a movement for a partner to copy or mirror. *Engage attention* by pointing out that their movement is affecting how their partner responds and moves. This is the basis of a *game plan* approach.

Extension
Move on to synchronisation. (The warm up here might involve 'mirror images' with one child leading and the other three copying in time.)

Triathlon 1

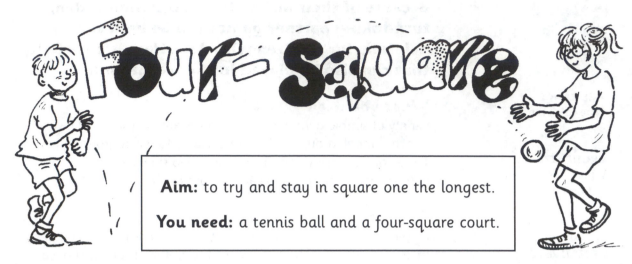

Aim: to try and stay in square one the longest.

You need: a tennis ball and a four-square court.

Making a four-square court

<table>
<tr>
<td>

1. Mark an 8m x 8m square with chalk on the playground.

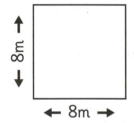

8m ↑↓ ← 8m →

</td>
<td>

2. Mark the halfway point along each of the four lines.

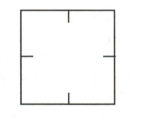

</td>
<td>

3. Draw lines across to form four squares and put the numbers in.

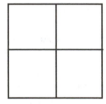

</td>
</tr>
</table>

How to play

1. Four players stand in each of the four squares.
2. The other players stand in a line waiting to go on.
3. The player in square 1 starts the game by hitting the ball with their hand into any other square so that it bounces in that square.
4. The player receiving the ball then has to hit it into any other square, to keep the rally going.
5. Play continues until either (a) a player misses the ball, (b) a player hits it so that it does not bounce in another square, or (c) a player allows it to bounce twice before hitting it.
6. If a player makes any of the errors above, they must leave the court and go to the end of the line.
7. The other players then all move up a place (for example, if 2 is out of the game then a new player comes in to 4, 4 moves to 3, 3 moves to 2 and player 1 stays where they are.
8. The player in square 1 serves again to restart the game.

Triathlon 2

Aim: to avoid getting hit below the knee, so becoming Kingpin.

You need: a soft football; a marked area roughly 10m x 10m.

How to play

1. Choose who is going to be Kingpin. If there are more than six players, you might have two Kingpins working together.
2. The Kingpin starts by throwing the ball underarm to try and hit a 'pin' (another player) below the knee.
3. When a player is hit, they are out and have to stand at the side of the court.
4. The game continues until there is only one player left. This player is then the Kingpin and the game begins again.

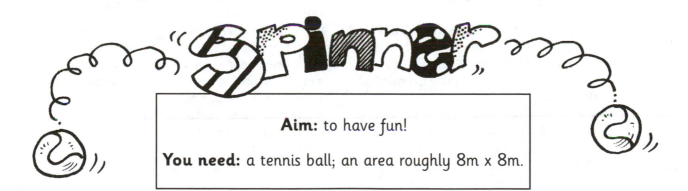

Aim: to have fun!

You need: a tennis ball; an area roughly 8m x 8m.

How to play

1. One player (the Spinner) stands in the middle of a circle or square with the ball. All the others stand around the edge.
2. The Spinner spins around and then throws the ball into the air, so that it lands in the circle or square.
3. The Spinner then shouts the name of another player and a part of the body, for example: 'Helen's left hand' or 'Tom's right leg!'
4. This player then has to run into the square and touch the ball with the correct part of their body before it bounces twice.
5. If they do not manage this, it does not matter! That player becomes Spinner and the play starts again!

RECOMMENDED RESOURCES

BOOKS FOR ADULTS
- *The Handbook of Autism: A Guide for Parents and Professionals* by Maureen Aarons and Tessa Gittens (Routledge).
- *A Structure for Success: Guidance on the National Curriculum and Autistic Spectrum Disorder* (ACCAC; visit www.accac.org.uk for more information)
- *Asperger Syndrome: A Practical Guide for Teachers* by Val Cumine, Julia Leach and Gill Stevenson (David Fulton Publishers).
- *Children's Letters* by Julie Garnett (Longman).
- *A Real Person: Life on the Outside* by Gunilla Gerland (Souvenir Press).
- *Autism: Handle with Care* by Gail Gillingham (Future Horizons).
- *Educational Provision for Children with Autism and Asperger Syndrome: Meeting Their Needs* by Glenys Jones (David Fulton Publishers).
- *Autistic Spectrum Disorder: Positive Approaches for Teaching Children with ASD* by Diana Seach (NASEN).

BOOKS TO USE WITH CHILDREN
- *Russell Is Extra Special* by Charles A Amenta III (Magination Press).
- *Idioms – Fun with English* by George Beal (Kingfisher).
- *The Penguin Rhyming Dictionary* edited by Rosalind Fergusson (Penguin).
- *The Snow Dragon* by Vivian French, illustrated by Chris Fisher (Corgi).
- *Diary and Letters Book* by Sue Palmer (TTS Group).
- *Little Rainman (Autism – Through the Eyes of a Child)* by Karen L Simmons (Future Horizons).

USEFUL ORGANISATIONS AND SUPPORT GROUPS
- Buzan Centres, 54 Parkstone Road, Poole, Dorset BH15 2PG (offers mind mapping courses, books and software for children). Tel: 01202 674676. Website: www.mind-map.com.
- EarlyBird Project, Hoylands House, Barnsley Rd, Silkstone, Nr Barnsley S75 4NG.
- The Hanen Centre (parent training and publications on the Hanen approach to language and communication): www.hanen.org.
- The National Autistic Society, 393 City Road, London EC1V 1NG. Tel: 020 78332299. Website: www.nas.org.uk.
- The Royal College of Speech and Language Therapists, 2 White Hart Yard, London SE1 1NX. Tel: 020 7378 1200. Website: www.rcslt.org.

USEFUL RESOURCES AND WEBSITES
- The Autistic Continuum: An Assessment and Intervention Schedule by Maureen Aarons and Tessa Gittens (nferNelson).
- Daily Life Therapy: www.musashino-higashi.org/english.htm.
- The Social Story Book and Comic Strip Conversations by C Gray (Arlington TX: Future Horizons).
- The Lovaas Approach: contact www.ulst.ac.uk for further information.
- MindManager software: for further information about contact Mindjet at www.mindjet.com.
- nferNelson: www.nfer-nelson.co.uk (send for a catalogue on specialist assessment).
- The Option Approach: www.option.com.
- PECS (Picture Exchange Communication System): www.pecs.org.uk/
- Harcourt Assessment: The Psychological Corporation, 32 Jamestown Road, London NW1 7BY. Website: www.tpc-international. com (send for the catalogue on 'Educational Assessment & Intervention').
- *More Than Words: Helping Parents Promote Communication and Social Skills in Children with Autism Spectrum Disorder* by Fern Sussman (Hanen Centre – available through Winslow Press, below).
- **TeacherNet**: practical guidance from the **Autism Working Group** is available through www.teachernet.gov.uk/wholeschool/sen/teacherlearning.
- **Winslow Press**, Goyt Side Road, Chesterfield, Derbyshire S40 2PH – send for the catalogue on 'Education & Special Needs' for various resources on autism. Website: www.winslow-cat.com.